DATE DUE

APR 1 0 1995	
MAY 2 3 1995	

DREAMS IN NEW PERSPECTIVE

DREAMS IN NEW PERSPECTIVE
The Royal Road Revisited

Edited by
Myron L. Glucksman, M.D.
and
Silas L. Warner, M.D.

 **HUMAN SCIENCES PRESS, INC.**
72 FIFTH AVENUE
NEW YORK, N.Y. 10011-8004

Copyright © 1987 by Human Sciences Press, Inc.
72 Fifth Avenue, New York, New York 10011

Printed in the United States of America
0 987654321

Library of Congress Cataloging-in-Publication Data

Dreams in new perspective.

    "This book is an outgrowth of a seminar, sponsored
by the American Academy of Psychoanalysis, in Philadelphia
on March 9, 1985''—Pref.
    Includes bibliographies and index.
    1. Dreams—Congresses. 2. Psychoanalytic interpretation.
I. Glucksman, Myron L. II. Warner, Silas L.
III. American Academy of Psychoanalysis. [DNLM:
1. Dreams—congresses. 2. Psychoanalytic Interpretation—
congresses. WM 460.5.D8 D7719 1985]
BF1078.D74   1987   154.6'3   86-28729
ISBN 0-89885-339-7

CONTENTS

CONTRIBUTORS

Walter Bonime, M.D.

Clinical Professor of Psychiatry, New York Medical College; Training and Supervising Analyst, Division of Psychoanalytic Training, New York Medical College

James L. Fosshage, Ph.D.

Board Director, The National Institute for the Psychotherapies, New York; Adjunct Associate Professor, Ferkauf Graduate School of Psychology, Yeshiva University; Core Faculty, Institute for the Psychoanalytic Study of Human Subjectivity (a specialty training institute of the National Institute for the Psychotherapies)

Myron L. Glucksman, M.D.

Associate Clinical Professor of Psychiatry, Yale University School of Medicine; Associate Clinical Professor of Psychiatry, New York Medical College; Training and Supervising Analyst, Division of Psychoanalytic Training, New York Medical College

Ramon Greenberg, M.D.

Visiting Professor of Psychiatry, Harvard Medical School (Massachusetts Mental Health Center); Faculty, Boston Psychoanalytic Institute

Stanley R. Palombo, M.D.

Clinical Associate Professor of Psychiatry, George Washington University School of Medicine

Montague Ullman, M.D.

Clinical Professor of Psychiatry, Albert Einstein College of Medicine

Silas L. Warner, M.D.

Dean, Philadelphia Academy of Psychoanalysis; Senior Attending Psychiatrist, Institute of the Pennsylvania Hospital

PREFACE

This book is an outgrowth of a seminar, sponsored by the American Academy of Psychoanalysis, in Philadelphia on March 9, 1985. If any one person was responsible for this event, it would be the late Leon J. Saul. For many years he taught a very popular class on dreams at the Philadelphia Psychoanalytic Institute. His systematic approach to the understanding of dreams and his particular interest in manifest content influenced many analysts in Philadelphia and elsewhere. He had the unusual ability to review a single dream or series of dreams during treatment, and to focus on the "red thread" of the patient's central psychodynamic conflicts, often facilitating a breakthrough when there was a therapeutic impasse.

The main purpose of this book is to broaden and enrich our theoretical and clinical understanding of dreams. Freud's brilliant *Interpretation of Dreams,* published in 1900, still remains the bible by which most psychoanalysts work with dreams. According to Freud's model, dreams are disguised attempts to fulfill sexual or aggressive wishes in order to preserve sleep. However, this theory does not take into account recent contributions from ego psychology, object relations theory, self-psychology, and interpersonal theory. Moreover, the data from sleep laboratory studies on the physiology of dreaming also need to be included in a contemporary psychoanalytic theory of dreaming. The papers in this book represent an attempt to accomplish this task.

We wish to acknowledge certain individuals without whose efforts the seminar and this book would not have been possible. Naturally, we are grateful to the authors of the papers who were so enthusiastic and cooperative in all phases of this joint project. In addition, we wish to thank Drs. Arthur Epstein, Spurgeon English, and Laurence Snow who participated in the seminar as discussants. We also thank the program committee that organized the seminar, including Dorothy Dewart, Edith Sheppard, Laurence Snow, and Hazel Weinberg. This group, along with the very able administrative director of the American Academy of Psychoanalysis, Vivian Mendelsohn, and her staff, provided the leadership that made the seminar the successful event it was. Finally, we wish to thank the faculty and candidates of the Philadelphia Academy of Psychoanalysis for their encouragement and support.

Myron L. Glucksman, M.D.
Silas L. Warner, M.D.

INTRODUCTION

The dream has traditionally been viewed as a unique clinical phenomenon ever since Freud's (1900) discovery that it is "the royal road to a knowledge of the unconscious activities of the mind" (p. 608). For nearly a century, *The Interpretation of Dreams* has remained the most influential publication in the psychoanalytic literature on the clinical significance of dreaming. In this monumental work, Freud not only explored the etiology and functions of dreaming, but he also introduced and further clarified some of the major foundations of psychoanalytic theory and technique. These included the nature of primary and secondary process cognition, the importance of infantile experience, the significance of repression, and the use of free association in the recovery of repressed memories. On the basis of his observations, Freud concluded that dreams are an expression of unconscious drives or wishes (sexual and aggressive) derived from our biological endowment and childhood experiences. He further postulated that the dream-work (condensation, displacement, and symbolism) constitutes a form of censorship or disguise of these wishes in order to preserve sleep. This model of dream formation (the so-called classical model) provided several generations of psychoanalysts with a rationale for the successful interpretation of dreams; that is, free association to the manifest content invariably leads to the dream's latent meaning and, ultimately, the impulses or wishes responsible for its formation. Although this was the nucleus of Freud's hypothesis, he also demonstrated how the dream can provide us with a wealth of clinical information regarding the patient's affective life, the impact of childhood events, the formation of intrapsychic conflict, the contribution of the id, ego, and superego to the latter, the various manifestations of resistance, and the nature of the transference.

Perhaps due to the sheer genius and magnitude of Freud's contributions, there were few modifications of the theory and clinical approach to dreaming for approximately 50 years following his initial observations. Some attention was given to the relative importance of manifest content, but the drive-discharge-censorship model of dreaming remained intact. The next giant leap in our understanding of dream function came from the sleep laboratory rather than from the consulting room. Aserinsky and Kleitman, (1953) Dement, (1955) and others demonstrated that a substantial portion of sleep consists of REM periods associated with dream activity. They observed that REM states occur in cyclical fashion throughout sleep and are correlated with repetitive, rhythmic, neuronal discharges orginating in the pons and spreading to the rest of the cortex. Moreover, although sleep usually persists during REM periods, it also continues throughout non-REM periods.

These observations not only suggest a biological substrate to dreaming which is necessary for homeostatic functioning, but they also cast doubt on Freud's (1900) wish-fulfillment hypothesis as well as his belief that "dreams are the guardians of sleep and not its disturbers." (p. 233). However, these findings do not refute Freud's essential discovery: dreaming mentation is different from waking mentation and has psychological meaning in terms of wishes, conflicts, feelings, self-representation, and relationships, as well as the continuity of past and present experiences. Nevertheless, the sleep laboratory data raise challenging questions concerning the biological and psychological functions of dreaming. What is the physiological purpose of dreaming, and does it have any relationship to the psychodynamic meaning of dreams? Do recent sleep laboratory studies require modification of the "classical" model of dreaming? The papers in this volume attempt to explore these questions as well as other relevant topics. The latter include a reassessment of the drive-discharge-defense model of dreaming in the light of new information derived from learning experiments, self-psychology, object relations theory, interpersonal dynamics, and cultural influences.

In general, there appears to be a shift in emphasis from the wish-fulfillment-censorship model to one that focuses more on the integrating, organizing, problem-solving function of dreams. This does not imply that wish-fulfilling and defensive elements are not present in dreams; rather, they are part of a more complex psychophysiological process which consists of a particular mode of mentation linking current and past experience for adaptational purposes. According to this model, the manifest content assumes greater importance as a metaphorical presentation of various intrapsychic issues. These include not only infantile wishes and the defensive processes they trigger, but also the regulation of affectively charged portrayals of the self and relationships with others (including the analyst), as well as attempts at problem or conflict resolution, whether or not connected with earlier childhood experiences.

Fosshage, in his chapter "New Vistas in Dream Interpretation," proposes a "revised psychoanalytic model" of
dreaming based on contributions from self-psychology and
object relations theory. In contrast to Freud, he views primary process (the predominant mode of mentation in
dreaming) not as a primitive form of mentation, but rather
as a highly complex activity consisting of visual and other
sensory images with affective colorations that serve an
overall integrative, synthetic function. He points out that
secondary process cognition also occurs in dreams in the
form of language and sophisticated conceptual operations
(e.g. mathematical solutions). He states that "the supraordinate function of dreams is the development, maintenance (regulation), and when necessary, restoration of
psychic processes, structure, and organization."

Fosshage believes that dreams do not always have a
latent meaning revolving around the censorship of sexual
and aggressive wishes. Instead, he suggests that rather than
being manifestations of disguise, dream images are metaphorical representations of affectively laden experiences,
narcissistically related issues, self-state, important relationships, and conflicts. For him, the conflict resolution
function of dreaming is not always defensive, but instead
also has the goal of new, constructive solutions and the
completion of developmental tasks. As a clinical example,
he presents two successive dreams of a patient in which
there is a gradual transformation of the patient's self-representation. Fosshage argues that conflict and defensive
functions are not the salient features of these dreams. In
summary, he states that in his revised model dreaming is
viewed as a highly developed, complex, imagistically dominated form of mentation engaged in developing, maintaining, and regulating psychological organization, including
conflict resolution.

Greenberg, in his contribution, "The Dream Problem

and Problems in Dreams,'' presents clinical and research data to support his view that dreams are attempts to integrate information from current experience and past memories in order to produce ''schemas'' that help the dreamer modify or adapt his behavior for the new demands of the environment. Greenberg reviews some of the experiments with animals and humans showing that REM deprivation impairs the learning of complicated tasks. He interprets these findings as evidence that REM deprivation results in an ''impairmant of adaptation.'' These studies suggest that complicated or ''unprepared learning'' requires the integration of unfamiliar information, and REM sleep appears to be necessary for this to occur. He points out that the evidence for drive-discharge as the motivating factor in dreaming has not been confirmed by the studies of REM sleep and REM deprivation. Instead of regarding the manifest content as a disguise for forbidden impulses, he suggests that it is a private, imagistic language portraying a particular issue or problem providing the dreamer with information from the present and past for the purpose of coping and resolution. Greenberg emphasizes that the manifest content is not an indifferent daily residue carrying latent infantile wishes, but represents through its metaphorical imagery the issues or problems with which the dreamer is struggling. Therefore, it is vitally important for the analyst to help the dreamer translate the imagery of the manifest content into waking language.

Greenberg describes an elegant experiment which he and his colleagues conducted in order to validate his ''problem-solving'' hypothesis of dreaming. This entailed correlating the material from analytic sessions with the content of REM periods collected in the sleep laboratory between analytic hours. They found a striking correlation between the problems or issues presented by patients in the analytic sessions preceding their dreams, and the problems

actually portrayed in their dreams during the night subsequent to their sessions. Of interest is their observation that
with the availability of transcripts of the analytic sessions
it became apparent that the dreams were easily translatable with little or no evidence of disguise. Greenberg then
presents the dream of one of his patients in order to illustrate the problem-solving model of dreaming. In conclu-
sion, he uses both laboratory and clinical evidence to
support his theory that the manifest content is a metaphorical portrayal of important problems or issues and attempts at their solution, rather than a disguise for latent
wishes.

   Palombo's chapter, "Can a Computer Dream?", ex-
plores dreaming as an information processing phenomenon
analogous to contemporary computer information systems. He points out that certain large computers integrate
new information into an organized long-term memory
structure at the end of the working day, which is similar to
dreaming when sensory input and motor activity are virtually blocked in contrast to the waking state. In dreams,
the day's significant events are matched affectively and
cognitively with earlier experiences and memories of a
similar nature. Long-term memory is "brought up to date
and enriched" by this process, and the dreamer gains further clarification or insight into his current life experiences
by means of this matching activity. Palombo continues the
analogy between dreaming and information processing
systems by stating that the "efficient distribution" of new
information into the system must be postponed until the
system is no longer in direct interaction with its environment (sleep). According to him, the drive-defense model of
dreaming is not supported by sleep research data, although
conflicts and defensive functions are evident in dreams.
Using the information processing model, the analyst can
help the patient understand how current experiences,

wishes, and conflicts are matched with related ones in the past. Both analyst and patient can then use this information to arrive at constructive resolutions.

Bonime's chapter, "Collaborative Dream Interpretation," focuses on the cooperative involvement required of the patient and analyst for the effective use of dreams during treatment. Bonime believes that working with dreams facilitates the patient's engagement in the analytic process, trust in the analyst, and familiarity with the method of free association in connection with dreaming and waking material. He emphasizes the importance of identifying and exploring affects in dreams so that the patient's personality can be more fully illuminated. Drawing on data from sleep, dream, and memory research, he speculates that the dream is "a state of pure free association" in which the associations are transformed into symbols and metaphors, creatively assembled and linked to recent and past experiences. Working together on dream content, the analyst and patient enhance their common storage of potentially useful information, and develop the capacity for the "reciprocal triggering" of relevant cognitive, mnemonic, and affective material. Bonime illustrates his point by describing the treatment of a patient in which their mutual associative and interpretive activity led to significant changes in the patient's behavior and functioning. He concludes by asserting that the analyst should not be confined to the role of interpreter, nor the patient to the role of free-associator. Rather, there ought to be a mutual associative, interpretive process with risk taking and collaboration in order to achieve a greater understanding of dreams, and to promote the personal growth of both patient and analyst.

In his contribution entitled "Manifest Dream Analysis in Contempory Practice," Warner emphasizes the clinical importance of manifest content. He reviews the evolution of psychoanalytic thinking on this topic beginning with

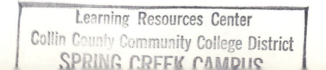

Freud, who believed that it was of much less significance than latent content in form and meaning. Subsequently, Erickson paid more attention to manifest content, and Spanjaard emphasized the conflictual material that it contains. Saul pointed out that manifest content represents a certain level of psychic activity that is both revealing and more acceptable to the patient, although still the product of unconscious forces. Kohut attached considerable importance to manifest content in regard to "self-state" dreams in which free association does not lead to further latent meaning other than that reflected in the manifest imagery itself. Warner reports the results of his survey of four psychoanalytic journals in terms of the use of manifest and latent content for dream interpretation. He found that manifest content was used for a significant number of dream interpretations by the authors. He then presents several patients and their dreams as examples of his use of manifest content for purposes of demonstrating clinical improvement in what he terms "turning point dreams." These clinical illustrations provide him with evidence suggesting that manifest content metaphorically presents the patient's conflicts, transference reactions, self-states, and other problems that make the pursuit of infantile sources redundant. He also points out that in addition to the clinical reasons for paying attention to manifest content, it can be utilized successfully in short-term dynamically oriented psychotherapy. In view of the ever increasing economic pressures to shorten the length of treatment, effective use of manifest content may be of practical value.

In the final chapter, "The Dream Revisited: Some Changed Ideas Based on a Group Approach," Ullman describes how small groups can facilitate the understanding and therapeutic application of dreams. He characterizes dreams as metaphorical visual displays based on current and past experiences which are "honest" portrayals of the dreamer's life. He believes that the group process can be a powerful instrument in promoting self-healing through working with dreams. Ullman outlines several stages in group dream work: in the first stage, the dreamer shares a dream with the group. Following this, group members offer their own projections in regard to the mataphorical meanings evoked by the dream imagery. During the third stage, the dreamer is given an opportunity to free associate to the dream at whatever level seems comfortable. Finally, a dialogue ensues between the dreamer and the group. Ullman believes that the lay public can be taught the necessary skills to engage in group dream work. He also suggests that it can be a dynamic and effective way for teaching psychoanalytic candidates-in-training a method of working with dreams. Ullman concludes speculatively that dreaming is concerned with the issue of "species-connectedness." He explains that while awake "we tend to lose sight of our basic interconnectedness" and focus instead on our individuality and separateness. While dreaming we have the opportunity to examine whatever may be interfering with our state of connectedness with others as well as with ourselves. Ullman concludes by wondering whether dreaming is "primarily concerned with the survival of the species" and only secondarily with the survival of the individual.

The panel discussion includes further elaborations on the contents of the presentations by each of the panelists. Considerable attention is paid to the similarities and differences between dreaming and waking mentation. Fosshage views dreaming mentation as a very sophisticated, highly developed cognitive-affective process. In his concept, it is not limited to conflict resolution or problem-solving activity, but also includes creative activity, new ways of organizing our perceptions, and attempts to restructure our internal psychic life. Palombo emphasizes that dreaming mentation has a two fold purpose: an adaptive, integrating function (conflict and problem resolution), and a defensive, regulatory function (neutralization of strong affects and threatening impulses). Ullman reminds us that dreaming is a primitive, life sustaining, biological function analogous to breathing. However, the psychological information provided by dreams can be used adaptively in our waking life. He points out that dreams reflect a more "honest" portrayal of ourselves than the "defensive expediency" we employ in our waking state. They enable us to see ourselves and our relationships from a fresh perspective in the simultaneous context of past and present.

Bonime emphasizes the importance of affect in dreaming mentation. He contrasts the integration of thoughts and feelings in dreaming mentation with that of waking experience; the former can provide us with valuable new insights into our behavior. Greenberg reports that dream activity occurs in both hemispheres according to recent studies of dreaming in aphasic individuals. He speculates that the "language" of the dream is mediated in a different area of the brain than is waking, spoken language. In general, the authors agree that dreaming mentation is multifunctional: it is adaptive, integrative, creative, and defensive. Manifest imagery is not only the product of defensive operations in response to sexual and aggressive wishes, but it is also a metaphorical presentation of all aspects of our psychic life: self-representation, feelings, conflicts, problems, interpersonal behavior, as well as past and present experiences. In summary, dreaming mentation regulates threatening impulses and feelings by means of its defensive operations, and facilitates the acquisition of new insights, fresh perceptions, and adaptive solutions to current dilemmas in the light of past experience.

The presentations in this volume are not meant to be a comprehensive review of dreaming. Our purpose has been to reexamine traditional psychoanalytic theory and practice in regard to dreaming, taking into account current research and clinical data. Clearly, many challenging, clinically relevant topics have not been addressed. These include an examination of the form and content of dreaming mentation in certain pathological states (borderline, psychotic, depressive). Another concerns the predictive accuracy of dreams in regard to analyzability and the potential for characterological change. Equally important is the value of sequential dreams in documenting evolving health, e.g. improvement of self-image, interpersonal growth, resolution of transference, and readiness to terminate treatment. Obviously, dreams include every aspect of personality development, structure, function, and psychopathology. They offer limitless opportunities to study key modalities of brain function: memory, cognition, affect, language, perception, and sensory experience. For the clinician and patient, they provide an unparalleled, occasionally puzzling, sometimes dramatic, always informative portrayal of our intrapsychic processes. They continue to serve as the royal road toward understanding ourselves and facilitating the growth of our human potential.

Myron L. Glucksman, M.D.

REFERENCES

Aserinsky, E., & Kleitman (1953), Regularly occurring periods of eye motility and concomitant phenomena during sleep, *Science, 188,* 273-274.
Dement, W. (1955). Dream recall and eye movements during sleep in schizophrenics and normals, *Journal of Nervous Mental Diseases, 122,* 263-269.
Freud, S. (1900). *The interpretation of dreams.* Standard Edition, (Vol. 5). London. The Hogarth Press, 1953.

CHAPTER 1

NEW VISTAS IN DREAM INTERPRETATION

James L. Fosshage, Ph.D.

Psychoanalysis has prized dreams for their revelation of profoundly meaningful psychological processes. In an attempt to understand dreams, different psychoanalytic models of dream formation and dream interpretation have emerged which, in turn, significantly influence the analyst's attention, organization, and interpretation of the dream data. As is well demonstrated in our study of interpretations of the same dream series by six well-known analysts (Fosshage & Loew, 1978, 1986), psychoanalysts usually perceive, understand, and interpret dreams quite differently, depending on their particular theoretical orientation and clinical approach to dreams.

Dreams, as is true for all psychological processes, are multiply determined and have multiple functions and meanings. In contrast to finding the "true" meaning of a dream, an analyst and analysand at best collaboratively hone in on the most salient meanings and functions of the dream. Our theoretical models of dream formation and dream interpretation provide an organizing function for this honing-in process. Because the observer, in this case the psychoanalyst, affects that which is observed, analogously to the well-known Heisenberg principal in physics, it behooves us to understand as well as possible the particular organizational dimensions of our theories. It is in this spirit that I wish to compare the classical or Freudian model of dream formation with a recently revised psychoanalytic model, which I have elsewhere set forth (Fosshage, 1983, 1986), emphasizing the primary organizing dimensions of these models and the differences in the methodology of dream interpretation.

THE CLASSICAL MODEL

As indicated by his choice of title and focus for his seminal work, *The Interpretation of Dreams* (1900), Freud placed dream interpretation at center stage of the psychoanalytic process. For Freud, the dream became "the royal road to the unconscious" mind which harbored repressed traumatic memories, infantile sexual and aggressive wishes, and unconscious conflictual processes. Freud perceived dreams as generated by sexual and aggressive impulses or their psychological representatives, infantile sexual and aggressive wishes, seeking discharge or gratification in the night. In order to find an avenue for discharge and yet still preserve sleep (since direct discharge would awaken the dreamer), these impulses or wishes attach themselves to a day's event, referred to as the day's residue, and are then disguised through condensation, displacement, and symbolization, the product of which is the final manifest dream.

In his attempt to understand the formation of the dream, Freud posited that in dreaming the mind regresses to an original (infantile) primitive mode of mentation, called primary process, whereby we are able to 'hallucinate' sexual and aggressive gratifications called wish fulfillments. Primary process is characterized as a primitive, free-flowing, i.e. energically unbounded, mode of mentation that never changes or develops. In contrast, the secondary process refers to the later and more highly developed conceptual, logical, and structured, that is, energically bounded, mode of mentation that uses linguistic symbols, and is more characteristic of waking thought. Since primary process is posited to be the predominant mode of mentation in dreams, the more developed forms of cognition have played a relatively minor role within this model of dream formation (refer to Fosshage, 1983, for a theoretical elaboration).

With the subsequent development of the tripartite structural theory (Freud, 1923a; Arlow & Brenner, 1964), dreaming has become viewed more as an expression of conflicts between three psychic agencies, that is, between the sexual and aggressive wishes of the id, the prohibitions of the superego, and the management functions of the ego. Although wish fulfillments remain an ever present thread in the fabric of dreams, it is posited that with few exceptions the central motif of dreams is conflict.

Using this model the primary task of dream interpretation is to reverse the dream formation process; that is, to undo the defensive processes in order to uncover the latent content, or the conflict involving infantile sexual and aggressive wishes, behind or contained within the manifest content. Freud (1923b) delineated the following techniques to use for this uncovering process: 1) obtain the patient's associations chronologically to elements A,B,C, etc., in the dream and obtain associations to these associations; 2) begin the associative work by selecting the most striking piece of the dream; 3) disregard the manifest content and inquire as to what events of the previous day might be associated with the dream; and 4) for those patients who are knowledgeable about the process, remain silent to enable spontaneous associations.

Because the manifest dream is viewed as a disguised product, the analyst working from this model does not typically perceive the manifest dream itself to be directly revealing of meaningful psychological processes. The manifest content is used primarily for eliciting associations during the decoding process. Despite a number of theoretical and clinical contributions substantiating that the manifest content is itself revelatory of meaning (Fairbairn, 1944; Erickson, 1954; Kohut, 1977), contributions which implicitly require, in my opinion, a radical revision of the classical model (see Fosshage, 1983, for details), the dream interpretive task of breaking through the manifest content to the meaningful latent content remains paramount within the classical model.

The primary organizing principle of this model is conflict involving infantile sexual and aggressive impulses and wishes, prohibitions and defensive operations. Accordingly, dream images are frequently *translated;* defenses are undone, into sexual and aggressive imagery with corresponding prohibiting forces and defenses, all of which is imbedded within the psychosexual developmental model. Interpretations often include translations of dream images into sexual organs and sexually dominated experiences. A sample is Altman's (1969) description of teeth:

> Without exception, when teeth appear in the manifest dream as a symbol, they refer to sexuality (often with aggressive connotations) in its latent content. The reference is to masturbation, intercourse, and, in women, to unconscious fantasies of pregnancy. Loss of teeth symbolizes the loss of the penis and fear of impotence. The dream marked by loss of several teeth accentuates the fear of castration. (p.22)

Dream figures are typically viewed as disguised representations of significant others and, with the focus on transference in the psychoanalytic arena, it is assumed that a transference figure latently appears in most dreams. Accordingly, translations of dream figures abundantly occur in interpretive formulations. Wishes and wish fulfillments, which at this point in the theory can emanate from the id, ego, or superego systems, are frequently ascribed to occurrences in a dream. For example, when there is a death in a dream, it is not uncommon for therapists to ascribe a death wish to the dreamer, whether it be toward himself or the other. When the dreamer is seriously abused in a dream, explanatory discussion often turns to latent masochistic wishes, in keeping with the aggressive drive-dominated theory of masochism. These formulations, based on the assumed ubiquity of defensive operations in dreams, require frequent translations of dream images and alteration of the dreamer's actual affect-laden experience in the dream.

Because the dream is viewed as a predominantly regressed product and the more highly developed cognitive functions, such as integration and conflict resolution, are by and large excluded from dream construction, the dream is viewed as expressive of only the conflict with minimal effort toward conflict resolution. Analysts using the classical model, therefore, consistently look to focus in dreams on the identification of conflicts, usually involving infantile sexual and aggressive wishes, the primary organizing dimension for the work of dream interpretation.[1]

[1] I am attempting to elucidate the primary organizing dimensions of the classical dream model that serve as the springboard for interpretations. Of course, clinically sensitive classical analysts, as other analysts, responding to the poignancy of the clinical material will deviate sharply from the model in their interpretive formulations. However, as with any science, these deviations need to be understood and formally included within our theoretical model to serve as a more accurate guideline for future understandings.

A REVISED PSYCHOANALYTIC MODEL

In order to integrate the more recent clinical and REM research findings, theoretical contributions in the area of dreams, and the current substantive theoretical developments in psychoanalysis (see Fosshage, 1983, for an extensive review), I have proposed a revised psychoanalytic model of dreams (Fosshage, 1983, 1986). In this model dreaming is viewed as a highly complex form of mentation which, occurring at night when direct involvement in the world is minimized, serves invaluable psychological functions. Primary process, predominant in dreaming mentation, is no longer viewed as an unchanging primitive mode of mentation, but rather is viewed "as that mode of mental functioning which uses visual and other sensory images with intense affective colorations [in contrast to the use of linguistic symbols of the secondary process] in serving an overall integrative and synthetic function" (Fosshage, 1983, p. 649).

We can refer to primary process as our imagistic or representational mode of mentation, corresponding with right hemispheric brain functioning (see Kinsbourne, 1982, for a comprehensive overview of right-left brain hemisphere research). Based on evidence derived from developmental and cognitive psychology (McKinnon, 1979; Lichtenberg, 1983) and the study of creativity and dreams (Noy, 1969, 1979), it is posited that primary process mentation as well as secondary process functioning can potentially, depending upon the particular life circumstances, increase in complexity throughout one's lifetime. Although primary process is the predominant mode of mentation in dreaming, in that dreaming typically occurs in images, secondary process or language appears in dreams and, at times, very sophisticated conceptual operations, such as the solution to mathematical problems, are carried out in dreaming mentation. Accordingly, it is posited in this model that *"the supraordinate function of dreams is the development, maintenance (regulation), and, when necessary, restoration of psychic processes, structure, and organization"* (Fosshage, 1983, p. 657).

Hence, dreaming is a mentational process occurring during sleep whereby we continue to assimilate and organize waking thoughts and events according to previously established organizational principles (or the thematic ways in which we organize our experience, Atwood & Stolorow, 1984) or through the development of new psychic configurations. For example, dreams may further the consolidation of emergent self and object configurations, a sense of self and a sense of the other. New incremental developmental achievements may be initially brought about through dreaming mentation.[2] One patient, for example, dreamed of confronting her intimidating and frightening father, a developmentally needed action. Previously, intense fear emerging out of her childhood relationship with her father precluded assertive action. The dream both momentarily expressed and contributed to the incipient intrapsychic changes in her sense of self, her image of her father, and the internal experience of their relationship.

Dreaming mentation often regulates various psychological processes, such as self-esteem, sexual and aggressive processes. Following a serious narcissistic injury, a

[2]Because higher order cognitive functions are excluded from dreaming mentation in the classical model, the psychological developmental function has gone unrecognized. In an effort, similar to this author's, to revise the classical model, Stolorow and Atwood (1982; Atwood & Stolorow, 1984) have independently emphasized the function of the consolidation and maintenance of organization. Apart from the classical model, Jung (1916) was the first to note the regulatory and developmental ("compensating" and "prospective") functions in dreams. Ullman (1959), French and Fromm (1964), and Jones (1980) have all noted the adaptive and conflict resolving functions of dreams.

dreamer might attempt to restore self-esteem through a dream scenario that involves a successful or self-enhancing action (what Kohut called self-state dreams, 1977). When sexual or aggressive affects have been stimulated and insufficiently managed during the day, these affects might be intensely expressed in a dream in a form that could be called wish fulfillment. However, wish fulfillment is no longer viewed within this model as a fantasied gratification of infantile sexual and aggressive impulses, as serving a primary function of discharge or as serving a defensive function, but rather as an avenue of regulation or management of these affect-laden experiences that contributes to the momentary completion of a psychological task and the restoration of psychological organization.

Yet sexual and aggressive acts occurring in dreams are not necessarily wished for or desired. For example, the dreamer's submission to a humiliating action, rather than a masochistically wished-for experience, can be understood, based on a different psychodynamic and developmental theory of masochism as well as a different dream model, as a repetition of a nuclear thematic experience, triggered by the previous day's events, that became established through the repetition of many such traumatic experiences long ago. Similarly, the death of an important person in a dream, in contrast to being the product of a wished-for aggressive act, may have been triggered by the threat or traumatic experience of a psychological loss or abandonment.

In addition to serving regulatory and developmental functions, "dreams continue the unconscious and conscious waking efforts to resolve intrapsychic conflicts through the utilization of defensive processes, through an internal balancing or through a creative, newly emergent reorganization" (Fosshage, 1983, p. 658). Dreaming is viewed within this model as a form of cognition, that includes highly complex cognitive functions and, thereby, continues and often furthers waking efforts at conflict resolution. Just as with our waking mentation, new solutions may emerge during sleeping mentation, accounting for the experience of entering sleep in conflict and waking up relieved with a new resolution and a renewed sense of direction.

The primary dream interpretive task from the vantage point of this model is to remain with, as closely as possible, the phenomenology of the dream: to understand the meanings of the particular images and experiences as they are presented in the dream itself. *Dream figures and images are typically seen not as the product of disguise, but rather as poignant organizational nodal points for particular affective reactions or thematic experiences.* Just as with waking thought, defenses may operate during dreaming mentation, particularly when intense intrapsychic conflict is present; but there is no reason to assume that defenses operate ubiquitously as the classical model posits (ibid., p. 652). Hence, a dreamer usually selects a particular dream figure, not to be a disguised stand-in for someone else, but rather because the figure within the dream context is a most poignant representative of the particular issues at hand.

In contrast to the assumption from the classical vantage point of the analyst's ubiquitous presence in dreams, the analyst within this model is never *assumed* to be present in the dream unless he actually appears. The same organizing principles or themes manifest in these dream experiences, of course, will be operative periodically in the relationship with the analyst (see Stolorow and Lachmann on transference as an organizing principle, 1984), but the analytic experience may or may not have triggered the concerns of the dreamer. If a particular theme is represented in the dream by a figure other than the analyst while it is simultaneously occurring within the transferential relationship, the theme within the dream and the transference can both be addressed without requiring a translation of the dream figure. Rather than a disguised stand-in for the analyst, the particular dream figure is viewed at that moment as a most meaningful representative of the thematic experience under consideration.

Without translations, dream figures can be better understood and appreciated for their significance. Only at those times when intense conflict involves defensive operations will it become apparent through the patient's associations that the dream figure is a product of displacement or other defensive measures. Working with the dream phenomenologically, in this manner, increases the dreamer's participation and conviction in the understanding of the dream and minimizes the potential for the analyst, within his role as the knowledgeable expert, to impose through translations of dream images his idiosyncratic ideas on the dream.

In order to understand a dream, phenomenologically associative activity is often initially more focused, as in the Jungian approach (see Whitmont, 1978). The aim is to elucidate and understand the affects, the images, the feelings toward self and others, and the primary themes between self and others as they appear in the dream. In order to understand the precipitants of the dream as well as to connect dreaming and waking life, investigation and associations move toward relating these dream themes to the dreamer's current waking life and, ultimately, to the historical and developmental context.

Since dreams are a form of cognition, they, as waking thoughts, vary in levels of complexity, clarity, and significance. If the meaning of a dream does not emerge clearly, the cause will not be ascribed necessarily to defensive operations, but rather to the possibility that the very issue may be, as of yet, unformed and unclear, just as in waking mentation. Variations in significance of dreaming mentation range from the emergence of a new psychological organization which substantially impacts and alters conscious and unconscious waking mentation to the simple completion of a comparatively mundane, but unfinished waking task. Consequently, in the latter case a so-called deeper meaning is not assumed, again in contrast to the classical model, to lie behind the manifest dream. Awareness of these variations in significance protects both analyst and analysand against a frustrating search for a "deeper meaning," against imposing "a deeper meaning" onto the dream, and against viewing the lack of deepening or productivity as the analysand's resistance.

Within this model, dreaming, rather than providing a royal road to latent wishes and intersystemic (id, ego, and superego) conflicts, is accorded a far more profound role in its developmental, regulatory, conflict resolving, and reorganizational functions. In turn, the model provides us with a greater range of organizational dimensions with which to approach and understand dreams. And the considerably decreased emphasis on defensive functioning and the corresponding manifest-latent content discrepancy enables us to observe more directly and clearly the meanings of the particular dream figures, images, and themes.

A CLINICAL ILLUSTRATION

Toward the end of a course on dream interpretation, a third year psychoanalytic candidate presented the case of Linda[3], which included two recent dreams. Both dreams dramatically show Linda changing in a profound way. The

[3]Certain details of this case have been altered to protect the anonymity of the patient. I wish to thank Joan Fromewick, M.S.W., for her cogent case presentation.

recognition of these changes, which aided their integration and consolidation, could not have occurred with the utilization of the classical model, but was facilitated with the revised psychoanalytic model. The discussion of the dreams is in no way intended to be exhaustive, but, paralleling the clinical situation, will focus on the most salient themes of the dreams.

Linda was a thirty-three-year-old, artistically inclined, single woman who held an administrative position in a small business. Her mother had suffered from a debilitating physical illness since Linda was nine. Throughout her childhood, her father had been an alcoholic and, when periodically enraged, had physically abused her and other members of her family. She had a younger sister whom, because of her mother and father's situation, she had often parented. She had entered psychoanalytic treatment for mental blocks in her work and interpersonal difficulties with men and with her superiors. At the time of the case presentation, Linda had been in treatment for over 2 years, primarily on a twice-a-week basis.

The first dream was as follows:

> The first part of the dream was a therapy session which we held in your apartment at your kitchen table. The walls were yellow and the room was sunny, and I felt happy, comfortable, and secure. At the end of the session, I went to the bathroom and found some of my clothes. I stuffed them into my pockets so that you wouldn't notice when I left.
>
> In the second part, I left your apartment. It was night and I found myself in a flimsy, tentlike cabin with my sister. We got into bed and a man came at us with a stiletto-like knife to rape and kill us. We wrestled with him and pushed him back. We went to the bathroom to clean off the blood and talked of how it was father's fault for not protecting us.

Linda felt that the dream was significant because this was the first time she had dreamed of her therapist. Next to the subject of sex, to talk about her feelings toward the therapist was the most difficult. She mentioned that she often felt vulnerable upon leaving the session (hence, needing clothes to cover up) and would go to the bathroom to "collect herself." Just recently she had been feeling more vulnerable because she remembered that her therapist had spoken of an upcoming vacation. At the next session she also mentioned that the dream helped because there were so many positive elements in it, even though it had turned into a nightmare.

As confirmed by her associations, Linda was in the process of integrating her increasing sense of comfort, support and security, emerging out of her experience within the analytic relationship. Accordingly, she could speak more openly about her relationship to her therapist and could acknowledge her vulnerability. The first part of the dream, in which she dreamed directly about her therapist, their relationship, and her experience within the ambience of the relationship, appears to express and to further consolidate the ongoing changes. However, outside the warm and protective relationship with the therapist, her earlier developed sense of vulnerability (partially related to not feeling protected by her father) reemerges ("flimsy, tent-like cabin with sister") together with the frightening object representation of the attacking man. It was unclear from the case material what had precipitated this reemergence of vulnerability and the frightening object representation although it might have been, in part, precipitated by her anticipation of the analyst's imminent vacation and the concomitant regression to the experience of the world as unsafe and attacking. Previously in therapy Linda typically had frightening nightmares in which men would brutally attack her. What was different about this dream was that Linda and her sister, with increasing psychological strength, were able to protect themselves and "to push him back," a newly developed capability that made the attacking man less terrifying.

At the next session Linda reported a dream from the previous night and initially associated it to a past dream:

> A long time ago I had a dream that I told you about. I was bringing my mother to my father. She was frail and I had to carry her, and I realized that was me — how I saw myself on the inside was that person.
>
> Well, I had another dream about that same person. Only this time I was off somewhere, but I knew my mother was pregnant. My mother was sick, like she is now; pretty helpless herself. I was trying to get home because I knew she was going to have the baby and I was in this hurried panic to get home. I had to be there when she had the baby. I got home. I was late and missed when she had this baby. I popped my head in to see if she was okay — a lot of people were around her. Immediately I went into the new baby's room, knowing that it was my baby; that I would have to take care of this child that my mother had; that the baby was completely my responsibility. There were no people in this room. The room looked a lot like a room in the house where I grew up. It had high windows, checkered curtains. I went to look at the baby. Things change in dreams. It went from a small baby to a larger one. I looked at it — pretty ugly baby. As I picked it up, its head fell back like a newborn's. I thought, "Oh, I forgot, I have to hold its head up." I started feeling more comfortable holding the baby, like I was remembering how. I looked at the baby, and it was me! And I was being very careful and very nurturing with this baby.

Linda mentioned that she smiled when she woke up. She then spoke: "The way I felt in the dream is kind of how I feel about myself. Like, I'm taking care of me and I can nurture myself. No longer do I have to look to my mother, because she can't be the mother, 'cause she's sick. And this little bitty baby — it was me. The me that always wanted to have a mother. And I was doing that myself. I never had a dream quite like that. I was just so tender. Like how I would really pick up a baby— really gently and, you know, a little awkward. I had to remember a few things and protect this baby. And instead of feeling this overwhelming responsibility, it was okay, and I knew how to do it. I mothered this child . . . ."

The analyst reported that she restrained her initial residual impulse to look for pathological conflict in the dream and found herself listening carefully to the mood and content of the dream which closely corresponded with her patient's associations. Linda spoke of "feeling better about herself," and of "having more compassion for the ugly baby inside of her" and "more ability to nurture it." "I'm more realistic in my evaluation of my own physical appearance." Whereas over the past 10 years Linda had made entries into her personal journal about "ghosts" which had "no substance" and which frightened her, now she saw "the ugly baby as something formerly a ghost" which is "now no longer so threatening that I can't own it as part of myself."

As a continuation of the developments of the previous dream, Linda in her dream and waking discussion was, within the ambience of an empathic therapeutic relationship, clearly in the process of acknowledging, accepting, nurturing and, therefore, gradually transforming her internal childhood self: ghosts without substance becoming an ugly baby in need of nurturance. With her newly discovered and developed resources, the responsibility of caring for herself, a previously burdensome task because of its prematurity, now was experienced as manageable and even desirable. The dreaming mentation was poignantly clear in both dreams, requiring no decoding (there was minimal defensive functioning), which enabled Linda to articulate comprehensively her understanding of the dreams with comparatively little needed from the analyst but affirming acknowledgment.

The developmental movements in these dreams are both expressed as well as further consolidated through dreaming mentation. Although the establishment of an empathic connection with and, thereby, a gradual transformation of previously negatively evaluated aspects of herself was undoubtedly brought about through the analytic work, the dreamer at this juncture is involved with internal changes, occurring within the empathic ambience of the therapeutic relationship, but not directly involving the analyst in her dream. Accordingly, at this moment no direct reference to the analyst is made in keeping with the dream content. Within the context of the self-selfobject connection within the analytic relationship, in this instance a "mirroring" connection (an acknowledging and affirming connection, Kohut, 1971, 1977, 1984), the patient is able to proceed with her internal transformation.

In contrast to the revised dream model, the classical model would not enable the recognition of these incremental developmental changes. The fact that Linda's waking associations confirmed her dreaming experience which portrayed the occurrence of profound intrapsychic changes precludes a meaningful application of the classical model, a model which does not account for or include developmental changes. Conflict, the essential ingredient of dreams within the classical model, is not a salient feature in either the initial section of the first dream or throughout the second dream.

However, conflictual processes involving aggression are clearly evident in the second part of the first dream. In contrast to the direct expression of the conflictual processes as viewed with the revised model, from the vantage point of the classical model the manifest scenario, a product of defensive operations, might be translated to emphasize the defensive management of the dreamer's aggressive drive impulses through the projection of aggression onto the attacking man and the scapegoating of her father. Such a formulation would belie Linda's dreaming and waking experience of the attacking man and, through the exclusive attribution of aggression to herself, could cause a serious empathic rupture, create considerable confusion, and potentially undermine her increasing capacity for self-protection. Similarly, in the application of the notion of wish fulfillment as a gratification of infantile impulses, Linda might be characterized as wishing for a supportive, comfortable therapeutic relationship, implying at best that this was not representative of her current experience and, at worst, that the wish is infantile and ultimately must be renounced. This formulation would clearly contradict her emergent experience in the analysis and, most significantly, in a regressive direction, i.e. the formulation would portray the patient as less developed than the evidence supports.

Although all analysts would attempt to understand the dream through the utilization of the dreamer's associational processes, our theoretical models provide readily available avenues for the organization of dream and associational material. In these particular dreams Linda's associations confirmed the developmental changes apparent in both dreams in keeping with the revised psychoanalytic model.

In addition, her associations to the conflictual section of the first dream elucidated the scenario as presented in the dream and did not point to the translation of dream images. Because the associations did not lead away from the manifest content of the dreams, the application of the classical model proved to be awkward, distant from the patient's experience, and void of meaning. In contrast, the application of the revised model accounted for or provided organizational dimensions in keeping with Linda's dreaming and waking experience, particularly with its emphasis on the manifest expression of meaningful psychological processes and on the dream function of the initiation and consolidation of intrapsychic changes in keeping with developmental strivings.

SUMMARY

A psychoanalytic model of the psychological function of dreams significantly shapes the analyst's attention, organization, and interpretation of dream data. The purpose of this paper was to set forth and compare the primary organizing dimensions of two models of dream function, namely, the classical psychoanalytic or Freudian model (Freud, 1900; Arlow & Brenner, 1964; Altman, 1969) and a revised psychoanalytic model (Fosshage, 1983, 1986).

Whereas in the classical model dreams are viewed as providing a wish fulfilling (discharge) function and as expressing intersystemic conflict, the revised psychoanalytic model posits that the function of dreams is to develop, maintain, and restore psychological organization. Whereas in the classical model of dreams defenses operate ubiquitously resulting in an omnipresent manifest-latent content distinction, within the revised model defensive measures creating a manifest-latent content discrepancy are viewed as operative only in response to particular instances of intense intrapsychic conflict. More typically, according to the revised model, dreams are directly revealing of psychological meaning.

Correspondingly, from the classical perspective the fundamental interpretive task for all dreams is to decipher the manifest content, that is, undo the defensive operations, to arrive at the latent meaning. From the perspective of the revised model the fundamental interpretive task is to elucidate and amplify the meanings of the dream images and themes. Working within the classical model usually entails translations of dream figures, which are seen as disguised representations of others and including a representation of the analyst. In contrast, working from the revised model requires a full amplification of the significance of the dream figures, for they are seen as important representatives of organizational nodal points.

Whereas within the classical model dreams are viewed as regressed primitive products, within the revised model dreams are seen as highly developed, complex, imagistically dominated mentational processes engaged in developing, maintaining, and regulating psychological processes and organization, including the function of conflict resolution. The recognition that dreams can incrementally further the consolidation of psychological organization in keeping with developmental strivings facilitates the use of dreams in analysis to enhance this consolidation process.

REFERENCES

Arlow, J., Brenner. C, (1964). *Psychoanalytic concepts & the structural theory*. New York: International Universities Press.
Altman, L. (1969). *The dream in psychoanalysis*. New York: International Universities Press.
Atwood, G., & Stolorow, R. (1984). *Structures of subjectivity: Explorations in psychoanalytic phenomenology*. Hillsdale, New Jersey: Analytic Press.

Erickson, E. (1954). The dream specimen of psychoanalysis. *Journal of American Psychoanalytic Association*, 2:5-56.

Fairbairn, W.R.D. (1944). Endopsychic structure considered in terms of object-relationships. In: *An object-relations theory of the personality*. New York: Basic Books, 1951.

Fosshage, J. (1986). *Dream interpretation: A comparative study*. (Rev. Ed.). New York: Spectrum Publications.

Fosshage, J. (1983). The psychological function of dreams: A revised psychoanalytic perspective. *Psychoanalysis and contemporary thought*. (Vol. 6). No. 4, 641-669.

Fosshage, J., & Loew, C. (1978). *Dream interpretation: A comparative study*. New York: Spectrum Publications.

French, T., & Fromm, E. (1964). *Dream interpretation: A new approach*. New York: Basic Books.

Freud, S. (1900). The interpretation of dreams. *Standard Edition*, 4 & 5. London: Hogarth Press, 1953.

Freud, S. (1923a). The ego and the id. *Standard Edition*, 19:3-66. London: Hogarth Press, 1961.

Freud, S. (1923b). Remarks on the theory and practice of dream interpretation. *Standard Edition*, 19:109-121. London: Hogarth Press, 1961.

Jones, R.M. (1980). *The dream poet*. Cambridge, Massachusetts: Schenkman.

Jung, C.G. (1916). General aspects of dream psychology. In *The structure and dynamics of the psyche. Collected Works*. (Vol. 8.), pp. 237-280, New York: Pantheon, 1960.

Kinsbourne, M. (1982). Hemispheric specialization and the growth of human understanding. *American Psychologist, 37,*4, 411-420.

Kohut, H. (1971). *The analysis of the self*. New York: Internaional Universities Press.

Kohut, H. (1977). *The restoration of the self*. New York: International Universities Press.

Kohut, H. (1984). *How does analysis cure?* Chicago: University of Chicago Press.

Lichtenberg, J. (1983). *Psychoanalysis and infant research*. Hillsdale, New Jersey: Analytic Press.

McKinnon, J. (1979). Two semantic forms: Neuropsychological and psychoanalytic descriptions. *Psychoanalysis and Contemporary Thought,* Vol. 2, No. 25-76.

Noy, P. (1969). A revision of the psychoanalytic theory of the primary process. *International Journal of Psycho-Analysis, 50;* 155-178.

Noy, P. (1979). The psychoanalytic theory of cognitive development. *The psychoanalytic study of the child.* New Haven, Conn.: Yale University Press, 34; 169-216.

Stolorow, R., & Atwood, G. (1982). The psychoanalytic phenomenology of the dream. *Annual of Psychoanalysis,* 10, 205-220.

Stolorow, R., & Lachmann, F. Transference: The future of an illusion. In press.

Whitmont, E. (1978). Jungian Approach. In J. Fosshage & C. Loew (Eds). *Dream interpretation: A comparative study.* New York: Spectrum Publications, pp. 53-78.

CHAPTER 2

THE DREAM PROBLEM AND
PROBLEMS IN DREAMS

Ramon Greenberg, M.D.

In 1916, Maeder, a Swiss psychoanalyst, wrote a paper entitled *The Dream Problem*. In that work, he considered modifications and additions to Freud's basic ideas about dream function and therefore about dream interpretation. In effect he suggested that Freud's approach led only to a retrospective interpretation of a dream. Maeder postulated that there was also a prospective aspect to dreaming that must be considered in the understanding of the dream. This view implied that the dream revealed the dreamer's efforts at adaptation to current emotional problems and the direction that might be taken in waking life. The dream also indicated the state of the dreamer in relation to his problems.

At the time, this was considered an heretical position. I will try to show how later studies of dreaming demonstrate that Maeder really was presenting a very prospective view of the process of dreaming. This approach is consistent with the ideas of later psychoanalysts such as French and Fromm (1964) and other contributors to this book. It fits well with findings that have emerged from sleep laboratories studying REM sleep in animals and humans and also with the exploration of dream material collected in the laboratory. Within a psychodynamic framework this leads to a greater focus on the manifest dream and on the language of the dream, which is drawn from the dreamer's waking experiences, both past and present.

After summarizing some of the earlier research, I will present data from studies by my colleagues, Drs. Chester Pearlman, Judy Kantrowitz, Anne and Howard Katz, Wynn Schwartz, and myself in which we focus on problems in the dream in a very literal sense. Some may find this simplistic when compared to the usual concepts of latent content and disguise, but I hope to show how this approach is just as meaningful as our traditional attempts at interpretation and also less arbitrary or open to multiple meanings.

As we consider these issues, it is worth keeping in mind the distinction Richard Jones (1965) makes between dream psychology and dream interpretation. The former involves the scientific study of dreaming and the latter the clinical process which searches for understanding of a particular dream. There is obviously an interaction between the two in that interpretation is usually based on some theoretical position and data from dream interpretation may be used in the formulation of theories about dreaming.

REM STUDIES

With this as an introduction, I will now describe some of the research that has led to our theoretical foundation for dream interpretation. In the late 1960s several investigators (Dewan, 1970; Breger, 1967; Newman & Evans, 1965; Greenberg, 1970) inspired by the newly emerging findings from the EEG study of sleep, suggested that REM sleep, that phase of sleep associated with dreaming, might play a role in the processing of new information. While these authors had similar ideas, there was little experimental evidence that bore directly on their hypotheses. They were reasoning from basic sleep research findings and from information gathered from earlier clinical psychological and computer experience. These hypotheses were important, however, because they gave direction to a series of experiments that explored the effects of REM deprivation on learning and adaptation. The findings were quite consistent and were replicated in a number of labs around the world. Studies (see Pearlman (1981) for a review) using rats and mice as subjects examined the effects of REM deprivation on various learning tasks. Some of these were one-way avoidance, the two-way shuttle box, latent learning of mazes, and discrimination tasks. The results of these studies showed that REM deprivation during training impaired the acquisition of the more complicated tasks while not affecting the simpler ones.

In a parallel fashion, studies (see Greenberg (1981) for a review) in humans examined the effects of REM deprivation on such tasks as learning word lists, creative thinking, adaptation to the viewing of an anxiety-provoking film, and performance on the Rorshach test. Here again, REM deprivation seemed to affect the more complicated tasks in a manner that could be interpreted as impairment of adaptation.

Based on the results of these studies, we have suggested that REM sleep is necessary for what Seligman (1970) has called unprepared learning while playing no role in prepared learning. Since the latter seems to depend on built-in instinctual patterns of behavior that are necessary for survival, it makes sense that an animal would not need to sleep on it in order to learn. However, the more complicated, unprepared learning requires some change in behavior involving integration of unfamiliar information, and here REM sleep seems to be necessary.

REM sleep is not only necessary for adaptation to these difficult tasks, but can be responsive to demand. When REM levels were measured during learning, an increase in REM occurred during the learning of those tasks that had been impaired by REM deprivation. Thus, during training for the two-way shuttlebox (Hennevin & Leconte, 1977) rats had higher levels of REM, students who showed improvement during an intensive foreign language course had increases in REM from baseline levels (DeKonnick et al., 1977), and subjects who were in a state of psychological disequilibrium had earlier onset of REM sleep than when they showed relative quiescence of conflictual activity (Greenberg et al., 1972; Greenberg & Pearlman, 1975).

I shall now try to demonstrate how the results of the REM studies can lead to a theory of REM function, and then how this can be applied to our clinical approach to dreams, by considering the dream as a manifestation of that function. Put simply, we see dreaming as integrating information from current experience with past memories in order to produce schemas that are organizers of complicated behavioral tasks. Thus, the dreamer can learn and modify or adapt behavior to new demands of the environment. This process can lead to a change in behavior or it can lead to the use of old patterns of behavior to cope with new situations. Furthermore, this process may be more or less successful. For example, the traumatic dream represents an instance of a failed dream because the new experience is not integrated at all. Instead, the traumatic episode is presented without any evidence of connection with other experiences of the dreamer.

APPLICATIONS AND ILLUSTRATIONS

If we now apply this hypothesis to dreams, the following ideas emerge. The dream shows how this process is
occurring. The content of the dream is a reflection of the issues with which the dreamer is struggling. It demonstrates
both the information from present experiences and from the
past. The information is expressed imagery that is part of
the dreamer's own private language (Greenberg & Pearlman, 1980) for representing a particular situation. The experiences that are usually the subject of the dream are those
that are problematic in the dreamer's current waking life.
The dream thus portrays problems and also the dreamer's
efforts at coping with these problems. Because this formulation does not take into account the traditional ideas of
disguise and latent content, we must digress a moment to
explain why these have been left out.

To begin, the evidence for drive discharge in dreams
has not been confirmed by studies of REM sleep and REM
deprivation. The idea of disguise derives from the notion
that it is necessary to hide the meaning of the dream in order to conceal the forbidden drives that seek expression.
Without the concept of drive discharge, the idea of disguise is no longer necessary. Latent content also assumes
a hidden meaning for the dream. We would suggest, instead, that the dream needs translation into our waking
language rather than requiring the uncovering of a hidden
meaning. In line with this thinking, we find that the manifest content is not an indifferent daily residue that is the
carrier of the latent dream wishes, but actually represents
issues with which the dream is dealing. Understanding of
the dream evolves from an understanding of the sources on
manifest content. Put another way, we ask what waking
experience the images in the dream are presenting. Thus we

are offering an alternative to the traditional approach to the dream and not just a negation of the classical theory and practice.

While we have formulated this approach on the basis of recent research, I would like to offer some other material to illustrate these points. My colleague, Chester Pearlman, and I reviewed Freud's Irma dream (Greenberg & Pearlman, 1978) with this in mind. We used information from Schur's paper on additional day residue for the dream (1966). This day residue involved the history of the surgical treatment of another of Freud's patients, Emma. What emerged was that the Irma dream contained, with amazing clarity, episodes from that unfortunate incident. Of importance in understanding the dream was the fact that the surgeon who had bungled was Fliess, Freud's closest and most idealized colleague. The dream then can be understood as Freud's effort to maintain his highly positive image of Fliess. This meaning is similar to Freud's interpretation of the dream but seems, when the source of the manifest content is taken into account, to capture more of the intense problem with which Freud struggled as a result of the Emma episode. In *The Interpretation of Dreams,* Freud (1900) focused on the idea of exoneration but he did not make the connection with Fliess.

Of course this formulation of Freud's dream is somewhat speculative, because we have no further access to the dreamer's thoughts. Let us, therefore, turn to some evidence from our research which is based on more complete data. We were fortunate to have the opportunity to have a patient, who was in psychoanalysis, come into our sleep lab for an EEG study of his sleep. During half the nights we awakened him at the end of REM periods for dream reports. Both the analytic sessions before and after each sleep lab visit and the dream reports were tape-recorded and transcribed. We thus had available an in-depth sample of the subject's waking mental life and extensive accounts of dreams. In an early study of this material, we found a marked correspondence between elements in the manifest dreams and elements in the analytic hours which were of clear emotional significance (Greenberg & Pearlman, 1975). The elements in the dream were direct representations of the waking concerns and required no interpretive activity. They were in effect pictorial portrayals of the analytic issues. For example, an hour in which the patient was concerned about regressing and becoming too dependent was followed by a dream in which the patient was in a car that threatened to slip back down a hill and that he was able to rescue by sticking out his foot and pushing forward.

In this first study, we looked mainly at isolated elements in the dreams. In our recent work we took more seriously the idea that dreams are struggling with problems. We therefore decided to score the dreams for problems and solutions and we also examined the analytic hours for problems. I will not go into details about our methodology, but should indicate that we were able to work out a reliable scoring system. In scoring the dreams for problems, we restricted ourselves to problems appearing in the manifest content of the dream. We, in effect, were taking our hypothesis seriously. We also assessed solutions on the basis of manifest content.

PROBLEMS AND SOLUTIONS IN DREAMS

Some illustrations will help demonstrate this approach. In the dream mentioned earlier, the patient was in a car driving up a steep and snow-covered hill. As he reached the crest, the car started to slip backwards. We scored the possibility that the car would slide back down the hill as a problem. The patient putting out his foot and pushing the car forward was seen as his solution. As the dream progressed, the patient seemed to be struggling with another problem, that of getting help. People were standing around and watching as he pushed the car over the top of the hill. As he put it, only when they saw that he had saved the car did they then hitch up an animal to help pull him.

In another dream, the patient was with a young woman and they were trying to make love. A dog kept barking at them and interrupting them. The disturbance by the dog was scored as a problem. They shooed the dog away. This was considered the solution. While all this seems rather simplistic, we feel it takes on more meaning when one looks at the analytic hours preceding the dreams. The problems in the dreams then stand out in their clear portrayal of the problems in the hours. In the first example, as mentioned earlier, the patient was preoccupied with his concern about slipping into a too dependent relationship to the analyst. He was quite anxious. The dream shows not only this problem but also a somewhat reassuring solution, which is to help himself and then get help. Of interest is the fact that this was a major feature of the patients's personality. Whenever he felt troubled, he would spring into action to prove to himself that he was in control.

The second dream shows a different problem. In the hour before the sleep study, the patient was talking about a trip he was about to take. A woman friend was going with him. He kept mentioning concerns about how he would perform sexually. Each time he raised such a question he would dismiss it with a comment to the effect that he didn't think he had to worry. The dream seems to be a continuation of his concern about disturbances of sexual activity, and the solution is also similar in that it involves shooing the disturbance away.

The differences in the quality of the solutions in these

two dreams should be noted. In our study we tried to assess the relative success of the dreams and then to evaluate the morning hours in terms of the kinds of problems that appeared. We wished to see whether dream "success" was followed by a change in the patient's ability to deal with a problem and hoped through this to demonstrate the overlap between understanding a dream and the function of dreaming. We will not consider the results of that part of the study in this presentation but instead will confine ourselves to the issue of understanding dreams in terms of the problems that appear in them.

The examples that I have given are illustrative of what we found in all 12 nights of dream collection. In each case the correspondence between the problems in the hours preceding the dreams and the problems in the dreams were readily apparent. Furthermore, the problems were seen as central in the analytic material. With the analytic transcripts available the dreams were easily translatable and showed no evidence of disguise. Put in another way, when one knows what is troubling the dreamer, an understanding of the dream becomes much easier. Thus, rather than ask what is the latent content, one can ask what is the source of the content of the dream. Associations become a way of going from the dream to what is meaningful to the dreamer. What we have found is that associations to the problem manifested in the dream become a powerful stimulus for eliciting material, from both the recent and the remote past, that is currently focal to the patient's concerns.

At this point it might be helpful to present a clinical illustration that will show how we can use the theoretical framework developed from the research we have been discussing.

In this example, the patient is a thirty-two-year-old woman who has been in once-a-week psychotherapy for about 3 years. Her major problems involve a chronic sense of depression and an inability to achieve fully the goals that she knows her considerable talents should make possible. She has made considerable improvement in how she feels about herself, but still finds herself struggling to go ahead. Recently, she was glowing with the prospect of having her first child, only to suffer a miscarriage. She seemed to be handling the disappointment quite well. In the process of dealing with the pregnancy she began to bring up a lot of material about her parents. They are two very disturbed people from whom she has had to gain some real physical and emotional distance in order to get on with her own life. In the interview preceding the one in which she describes her dream, she was talking about her father and some of his recent psychotic responses. She then brought in a dream which is as follows:

She was in England, in the yard of a beautiful house. The weather was warm and sunny and the garden lovely. Her father was there. She became very sad as she began to think that her father was soon going to die. She also kept hearing the music of Loch Lomond, *verse after verse, until she could no longer stand it and woke up.*

We talked about the problem manifested in her dream which was her sadness at the thought of losing her father in the context of this wonderful setting. She then began to bring up memories with an affect she had never clearly shown before. This was a sense of pride and admiration for her father. These memories were from her early years, when they lived in the country. At that time, father was eccentric but not yet sick. She described how he could make and fix all kinds of things, and how she used to follow him and help him. He also used to sing a tune over and over. This all changed when he got a better job and they moved. After that he became sick and she and her sister felt as if, in effect, they had no parents. When I commented that he really had died then, she was very sad as she agreed that was so. Of course the words of *Loch Lomond* capture this loss of love poignantly. We were then able to consider how her feelings about his failure were related to some of the difficulties she was experiencing with being successful. In this example, I have tried to illustrate an important feature of our approach to dreams. This is the assumption of the focusing power provided by calling attention to the problem in the dream. The associations to this problem are then associations to what is currently of major importance to the dreamer.

THE MANIFEST DREAM: DISGUISE OR PORTRAYAL?

I have tried, in this presentation, to indicate how the results of recent sleep research have led us to reconsider the way we understand the process of dreaming and how we approach the dream in the clinical setting. It is important to underline the fact that we retain some of Freud's basic ideas, specifically that the dream has meaning and that this meaning is related to what is emotionally significant to the dreamer. However, we then depart from classical psychoanalytic dream theory and practice in that the manifest dream is seen as a portrayal of what is important rather than as a disguise. The dream represents both the problem with which the dreamer is struggling and the efforts at solution. The latter may be more or less successful. Work with the dream in the clinical situation involves understanding the source of the problem in the dreamer's waking life and also that the reasons for the emotional significance of the problem come from the patient's past life.

As we have considered this approach to the dream, we have also been struck by the congruence of this way of understanding of the dream with many of Kohut's (1977) ideas about self-psychology. The dream can be seen as a means for integrating emotionally meaningful experiences so as to maintain a continuity or cohesiveness of one's sense of self. The focus is on what the patient is experiencing both in the dream and while awake and the assumption is that there is an essential connection between the two.

We also feel that we are more closely in touch with the patient than if we begin to look for more metapsychological meanings in the dream. The latter approach often leads to many different interpretations all of which *might* be right. I should also mention that many experienced clinicians may find themselves dealing with dreams in much the same manner that we have described. They hold on, however, to a theory of dreaming that does not explain their activity in a very coherent way. I hope the ideas presented here can provide some congruence between our theory of dreaming and our clinical use of the dream, and that dream problems can help us with *"the dream problem."*

REFERENCES

Breger, L. (1967). Function of dreams. *Journal Abnormal Psychology Monograph 72:* No. 5: 1–28.

DeKonnick, J. Proulx, G., King, W., & Poitras, L. (1977). Intensive language learning and REM sleep. *Sleep Research 7,* 146.

Dewan. E. (1970). The programming (P) hypothesis for REMS. *International Psychiatric Clinics 7,* 295–307.

French, T., & Fromm, E. (1964). *Dream interpretation: A new approach* New York: Basic Books.

Freud, S. (1900). *The interpretation of dreams* S.E.4.

Greenberg, R. (1970). Dreaming and memory. *International Psychiatric Clinics 7,* 258–267.

Greenberg, R. (1981). Dreams and REM sleep—An integrative approach. In W. Fishbein, Ed. *Sleep dreams and memory.* New York: Spectrum Publications.

Greenberg, R., Pearlman, C., & Gampel, D. (1972) War neu-
roses and the adaptive function of sleep. *British Journal of
Medical Psychology* 45, 27–33.

Greenberg, R., & Pearlman, C. (1975). REM sleep and the analytic process: A psychophysiologic bridge. *Psychoanalytic
Quarterly 44,* 392–402.

Greenberg, R., & Pearlman, C. (1975). A psychoanalytic dream
continuum: The source and function of dreams. *International
Review of Psychoanalysis 2,* 441–448.

Greenberg, R., & Pearlman, C. (1978). If Freud only knew: A
reconsideration of psychoanalytic dream theory. *International
Review of Psychoanalysis 5,* 71–75

Greenberg, R., & Pearlman, C. (1980). The private language of
the dream. In J. Natterson, Ed. *The dream in clinical practice.*
New York: Jason Aronson.

Hennevin, E., & Leconte, P. (1977). Etudes des relations entre
le sommeil paradoxal et le process d'acquisition. *Physiological Behavior* 18:307–319.

Jones, R. (1965). Dream interpretation and the psychology of
dreaming. *Journal American Psychoanalytic Association, 13,*
304–319.

Kohut, H. (1977). *The restoration of the self,* New York: International Universities Press.

Maeder, A. (1916). The dream problem. *Nervous and Mental
Disease Monograph* No. 22. New York: New York Publishing
Co.

Newman, E.A., & Evans, C.R. (1965). Human dream processes
as analogous to computer programme clearance. *Nature 206,*
534.

Pearlman, C. (1981). Rat models of the adaptive function of REM
sleep. In W. Fishbein, Ed. *Sleep, dreams, and memory.* New
York: Spectrum Publications.

Schur, M. (1966). Some additional 'day residues' of the 'specimen dream of psychoanalysis'. In R. Lowenstein et al. (Eds.)
Psychoanalysis—A general psychology New York: International Universities Press.

Seligman, M. (1970). On the generality of the laws of learning.
Psychological Review 77, 406–418.

CHAPTER 3

CAN A COMPUTER DREAM?[1]

Stanley R. Palombo, M.D.

At first glance, dreaming may seem less like computation than any other activity of the human mind. The im-
pressive achievements of artificial intelligence research
(Boden, 1977; Dennett, 1978; Simon, 1981) have shown that
computers, when expertly programmed, can perform in a
way that closely resembles rational thought in humans. But
dreaming has alway been the exception to the rule of reason in mental life. The dream has been seen as the medium
of the irrational, of the wild and willful elements in human
nature, if not of a supernatural intrusion into the human
world. Subjective experience tends to confirm these primitive impressions. To the dreamer, dreaming seems not only
disorderly but defiantly so.

Psychoanalysis, of course, has mitigated this extreme
view. It has demonstrated that beneath the apparent defiance of order, dreaming is both meaningful and motivated.
However, the traditional psychoanalytic theory of dream

[1]This paper was previously published in the *Journal of the American
Academy of Psychoanalysis,* Volume 13, No. 4, pages 453–466, Octo-
ber 1985.

construction does not locate these elements of meaning and motivation in the actual content of the dream, but in the dreamer's associations. For the traditional theory (Freud, 1900, 1917), the manifest content is an unstructured conglomerate of disconnected fragments, accidentally thrown together by the thrust of irrational forces.

Meaningful and motivated mental activity is by nature computational. Even the expression of the most primitive impulse requires the matching of an inner mental schema of the desired object with the real objects actually available in the outside world. The matching process itself, even at so simple a level, is a form of computation (Palombo, 1980).

The short answer to my question today is therefore that all of our dreaming is done by computer, the same biological computer that does the rest of our daily information processing (Lindsay & Norman, 1977; Sowa, 1984). But the point of my discussion will be to go beyond this truism to show that under similar circumstances, man-made computers also exhibit dreamlike behavior, and that when they do, they conform to the same general information-processing rules and constraints that apply to human dreaming.

Sleep research in laboratory animals and humans (Fishbein, 1981; Scrima, 1982) has shown that dreaming sleep (usually referred to in the literature as REM or rapid eye movement sleep) is necessary for the transfer of new experiential information from a temporary short-term memory structure that collects the events of the day into permanent long-term storage. My earlier work suggested that when human beings dream, new experiential information is matched through the mechanism of condensation or comparison by superimposition with related experiences already stored in long-term associative memory (Palombo, 1976, 1978). Dramatic physiological changes take place during dreaming sleep to isolate the dreamer from the outside world while his sensory projection mechanisms are employed in this highly specialized way.

All mammalian groups undergo the same physiological changes during REM sleep. Relatively complex precursors of the dreaming state must have existed in pre-mammalian forms, but without the availability of a clear-cut behavioral tracer like REM sleep it is difficult to follow the history of these precursor states before the advent of the mammals. With the evolution of large computer information systems as a model, however, we can reconstruct the development of dreamlike information processing states from their most rudimentary beginnings.

What I propose to do here is to examine the evolution of dreamlike processes associated with memory allocation and organization in the simple computers of a generation ago and in one of the largest and most complex computer information systems in operation today. This latter system, which I will describe further on, is still very far from reaching the functional level of a marsupial. Nevertheless, the developmental line it has taken is pointing clearly in the direction of human dreaming.

The essential point of similarity is that in computer systems, as in the human brain, the processing of information for direct interaction with the environment is separate and distinct from the processing of internally stored information. In the first case, the goal is an action that will alter the relationship of the system to the outside world; in the second, it is the reorganization of internal structure. For the large contemporary computer system, the collection and initial registration of new information takes place during business hours, in the midst of a pressured interaction with a demanding environment, but the integration of this new information into an organized long-term memory structure cannot be carried out until the interaction with the environment has been shut down at the end of the working day. This directly parallels the physiological changes during the dreaming state in the human, where sensory input is blocked and the voluntary muscular system is almost completely inactivated, so that interaction with the outside world is reduced to the bare minimum necessary for physical safety.

DREAMING AND MEMORY

The coincidence of REM sleep with the experience of dreaming was discovered more than 30 years ago (Aserinsky & Kleitman, 1953; Dement, 1955). Freud had suggested that a dream originates at a particular moment when a long repressed infantile wish breaks through the defensive barrier of the unconscious and manifests itself in disguised or distorted form in consciousness. But it was found in the laboratory that dreaming sleep is a cyclical phenomenon. It takes place in roughly equal periods of about 20 minutes, occurring regularly at intervals of 90 minutes all night long. Freud's hypothesis that the individual dream is initiated by an isolated unconscious impulse had been disconfirmed.

A dream is the product of a dream-generating system that works on a regular schedule, without regard to the frequency or intensity of unfulfilled wishes. Dreaming is an ongoing mental process essential to the well-being of the dreamer. Lowy (1942), elaborating on an idea of Bjerre's (1936), had proposed such a process more than a decade before the discovery of REM sleep. He suggested that the primary function of dreaming is to establish meaningful connections between the dreamer's present life concerns and related events recorded in the distant past, and now inaccessible to his waking consciousness. This function, he said, is accomplished entirely during sleep. The recollection of a dream in waking consciousness allows the dream materials to take part in a self-reflective or interpretive process that is not intrinsic to its more basic primary function.

Lowy's idea that the primary function of dreaming is more primitive than the self-reflectiveness of waking human consciousness was supported by the laboratory finding that REM sleep is present in mammals generally. Bjerre had suggested (Lowy, 1942) that "by means of the dream formation, details of the past are continually re-introduced into consciousness," and that when "the connection function of the dream-formation . . . condenses masses of experiences, perhaps a whole period of a dreamer's life, into one single image, then all the material which is contained in the synthesis is reconnected with consciousness" (p. 201).

The data of the sleep laboratory showed that Lowy was correct in thinking that the dream ordinarily takes place in a state of mind different from ordinary consciousness. Only a small fraction of dreams are ever remembered by the dreamer, and only those from which the dreamer has momentarily awakened. Only if the dreamer is awakened within 5 to 10 minutes after the end of a REM period can he recall anything of the dream's contents (Dement & Wolpert, 1958). It had become apparent that the connecting function of the dream formation is operating below the level of waking consciousness.

LONG- AND SHORT-TERM MEMORY

What were the past events recovered in the dream being connected with, then, if not waking consciousness?

Evans and Newman (1964) had suggested that dreaming is like the printout of a large computer's memory contents, an incoherent jumble of apparently unrelated elements. Reviving an older theory of Robert (1886), they proposed that in dreaming, the previous day's experience is being eliminated to make room for the new experience of the following day.

The contents of a dream are not an incoherent jumble, of course, but an intricate structure of intersecting associations. Dreaming was not discarding the contents of daytime processing, but carrying it further in a different way. The computer analogy was particularly apt, however, in its suggestion of a discontinuity between the memory structures appropriate for temporarily storing the masses of new information taken in during the day and the rather different structures needed for storing information over the very long term. Before the computer, it had been possible to believe that *all* experience could be effectively stored in long-term memory, even if much of it remained inaccessible because of repression and the other mechanisms of defense. But the management of memory structures is a significant aspect of the mental economy. The storage of even the very smallest unit of information has a price in the computer, and the storage of masses of information in the brain must also be subject to important limitations.

Freud had had a striking intuition into the two distinct phases of memory, reported in his 1925 article, *A Note Upon the Mystic Writing Pad*. The mystic writing pad is a familiar toy. Figures can be drawn on the pad with a stylus and then made to disappear mysteriously by lifting the top sheet. In this famous paper Freud had compared the workings of the human memory to the two distinct forms in which an impression is registered on the pad. With the translucent gray top sheet blank, a new figure can be drawn with the stylus, by pressing the gray sheet against an underlying resinous black surface, which then shows through the upper layer only where pressure has been applied.

When the top sheet is lifted, the figure disappears from it, but an impression of it remains permanently in the black underlayer, indistinctly merged with all the impressions that had been laid down previously. According to Freud, the registration of the day's events in human memory was like the drawing of the figure on the top sheet of the pad. The permanent impression left by those events in the unconscious was like the confused mass of superimposed impressions on the black underlayer.

Hawkins (1966), Greenberg and Leiderman (1966), Breger (1967) and Dewan (1967) all picked up the similarity between the short-term memory of the computer and the record of the day's events in the human memory as it was represented by the upper layer of the mystic writing pad. But instead of seeing dreaming as the emptying out of the daytime memory, like Robert and Evans and Newman, they saw it as the process through which the events of the day are integrated into the structures of long-term memory, where they leave a permanent impression.

The "connections" described by Bjerre bring together the significant events of the dreamer's current life situation and the early memories retrieved from long-term storage matched with them in the composite imagery of the dream. An important part of the analyst's job is to recover these significant events from the innocuous substitutes introduced by the dream censor.

The transfer of new information from short-to long-term memory is not a physical movement but an associative integration of the new events into an already very complex and elaborate structure. Both the short-term and long-term interests of the dreamer are advanced by this procedure. Long-term memory is brought up to date and enriched by new experience. At the same time, the significant events of the dream day are illuminated when viewed in the context of similar events whose consequences in the past have already been recorded and integrated into the dreamer's repertoire of gratification-seeking activities.

As a representation of the contrasting features of short- and long-term memory structures, the layers of the mystic writing pad serve surprisingly well. For a simple organism, or any system dependent on information from its environment, a short-term memory structure must be able to contain an accurate mapping of its immediate surroundings. Impressions stored in this structure must be precisely outlined and distinct from one another. Sharp detail is necessary to allow the organism to orient itself with respect to the dangers and opportunities in its neighborhood, but relations among the various impressions are less important than their individual features.

Short-term memory is designed for interaction with the outside world in real time. It need not extend very far back into the past. A period of hours may be enough to track the movements of predators and prey while they are nearby. *Access* to the information in short-term memory must be extremely rapid, however, since events often take a sudden course and shifts of trajectory must be plotted instantaneously.

Long-term memory is quite different. Like the underlayer of the mystic writing pad, it contains the superimposed records of events originally separated in time. Its structure is determined by the common elements shared by these superimposed impressions, rather than by the details of individual events. Simple organisms and small information systems can do without it.

Where short-term memory is critically tied to chronology, long-term memory is indifferent to it. Very little depends on the actual lapse of time between the recording of events related through their cognitive or affective significance. If we read out the contents of long-term memory, as we can do on occasion when we hear a patient's associations to a dream, we experience the sense of timelessness that struck Freud with such force.

Short-term memory contains a great deal of detailed information about relatively few events; long-term memory relatively little information about many events. Before the information in short-term memory is transferred to long-term, it must be sorted out and selectively reduced. Then it must be matched with events already contained in long-term storage.

THE COMPUTER MEMORY

The history of computer information systems illustrates how practical considerations dictate the division into short- and long-term memory structures. In the earliest and simplest computers, effective problem solving required only a reusable, rapidly accessible short-term memory just large enough to store the operating program and the intermediate results of its computations. Access to this structure had to be on the scale of microseconds to prevent interruption or delay in the operating cycle of the computer.

Long-term memory was needed when large and unpredictable quantities of data were to be processed and the results of the processing permanently stored. Recording and retrieval operations are infrequent and intermittent relative to the operating cycle. Rapid access to long-term storage, while desirable, is not a critical factor. The ability to add new storage space as the results of the computation accumulate is more important.

In the simplest computer, recording and retrieval to and from mass storage media can take seconds rather than microseconds to complete. While it goes on, the central processing unit of the computer simply waited. As computer systems increased in size, it became necessary to use this otherwise wasted computing time. A major advance in computer evolution took place when it became possible to program the computer to occupy itself on a series of independent tasks while waiting for access to the mass storage devices.

INTERACTIVE AND BATCH PROCESSING

Short-term memory, with its rapid retrieval time, optimizes the efficiency of the computer for its own internal problem solving. The interaction of the computer with the single human user was still relatively inefficient, however, because the reaction times of human and computer are quite different for different tasks. Both the user and the computer must be idle for much of the interaction as each waits for the other to catch up.

In the days when the computer's time was much more valuable than the user's, it was customary to minimize their interaction by having the user enter his instructions and data as a set of punched cards placed in a stack for later execution. The computer would run through a batch of these programming tasks before any of the users could see his results. Because the backlog of work to be done increased during the day and fell off during the night, the user would often have to wait until the next day or even longer to see whether his program was working correctly. If he found a problem, he would have to repeat the entire procedure.

Interactive processing, though wasteful, is more convenient for the user. He can run the program, diagnose the errors, and make needed corrections all in a few minutes. He can work with the computer on his own real time scale, a great advantage. When the computer was involved with the user in making critical split-second decisions, as, for example, in the guidance of a spacecraft in flight, interactive processing was essential.

By the late 1950s, large computers were already extremely fast, fast enough to be programmed to interact with many users simultaneously in their own time. Each user could work independently at his own speed, while the computer was busy with the others. Mass storage devices could be accessed rapidly enough to be incorporated into the short-term memory available to the human user. One of the first complex multiuser programming systems with these capabilities was RTOS, an interactive real time operating system originally developed by NASA from the Project Mercury guidance system. The nationwide airline reservation system, developed at about the same time, was another large interactive system.

Interactive processing allows the computer system effectively to answer a multiplicity of external demands, like the simple organism we spoke of earlier. In the next stage of its evolution, we find a computer information system capable of storing the individual transactions of hundreds of daily users and reorganizing these records in a variety of ways at night.

A PARTIALLY EVOLVED
COMPUTER INFORMATION SYSTEM

AAS is the acronym for the Advanced Administrative System of a very large manufacturing concern (Wimbrow, 1971). In continuous operation since 1968, by 1974 AAS was already interacting with more than 1500 terminals throughout the United States. At that time it was performing 20 major business functions for the corporation. It took

new orders, transmitted them to production, billed cus-
tomers according to a variety of payment and leasing
schedules, and kept track of maintainence charges for the
original equipment and for additions and modification made
to it at various times.

Apart from modification of the system programs, AAS
was originally designed to operate exclusively in real time.
The design was quickly modified, however. It was found
that the procedures for organizing and updating long-term
memory could operate efficiently only when the interactive portion of the system was completely shut down, exactly as it is in the human during REM sleep. Like mass
storage devices in the earliest computers, batch processing
supplied a major element in the information background
essential for effective processing in real time.

AAS has gone through a complex evolutionary process of its own. Several generations of new and more powerful computers have been added to it, along with more
complex and comprehensive programming tools. For example, when AAS came into operation it used NASA's
RTOS for its real time interactions, but this was soon re-
placed by a more advanced system designed specifically for
the IBM 360 computer. Like an organism, AAS has had to
undergo major alterations without interruption of its regular routine of interactive functions. A number of planned
improvements in the system had to be postponed or rejected at various times because they could not maintain
operational continuity with the older system.

AAS used several large computers to process incoming messages. Since these computers all required access to
a common long-term memory store, it was necessary to
prevent them from trying to retrieve or store information
from a particular file in long-term memory at the same time.
A "front-to-back" design was found to be the most efficient for dealing with this problem. The long-term memory

store, the "back end" of the system, was given its own computer for processing and reordering the incoming calls from the computers comprising the "front end."

Even with this arrangement, however, it was impossible to keep the long-term memory up to date during the hours when the users were interacting with the system. To integrate the newly recorded information into long-term memory, it was necessary to organize it hierarchically into levels of records, strings of records, groups of strings, and, finally, about 200 large units called files. Each of these levels had its own method of indexing. According to Wimbrow (1971), during the working day:

> New records added to the file are placed in an overflow area specifically set aside for that purpose. Index records are created and/or modified to logically integrate the new records into their respective files. This is one of several housekeeping functions that are scheduled in a batch mode when the terminal network is shut down. From time to time, it is necessary to reorganize the files because additions and deletions eventually distort their physical sequence to such an extent that retrieval time is adversely affected. Reorganization is accomplished by rewriting the data records in their proper sequence in another location and eliminating the original file storage area. The index files that refer to the reorganized data files must also be recreated so as to point to the new locations. (p. 277)

Among the "housekeeping functions" carried out during nightly batch processing are balance and reconciliation routines that search the daytime activity file for errors and inconsistencies and match them against the records already in long-term memory. There are also a number of crossfile updating programs. Some transfer whole files of information routinely collected during the day into a new sector of long-term memory. For example, the record of the day's product shipments is read into the billing files for billing action on the following day.

Changes made in the price file during the day are distributed to the various inventory files at night. Still other programs check to see whether any of the modifications made during the day in individual files need to be copied into other related files. Changes in the order files, for instance, are copied into the inventory files during the night. More than 50 batch programs are involved in transferring the data collected during the day into long-term memory and then redistributing it according to the needs of the system as a whole.

Compared with our own information processing needs, the work performed by AAS is extremely primitive. It is apparent, however, that in a rudimentary form the nocturnal batch processing of AAS has already acquired the functional outlines of mammalian dreaming. The designers of AAS did not set out to imitate the information-processing methods of the human mind. Unlike researchers in artificial intelligence, who attempt to model their programs after human mental processes, the creators of AAS were trying to do a difficult job in the real world, with economic considerations uppermost in their planning.

As the system became more complex, pressure was repeatedly applied by the user community to reduce the batch processing phase. Nevertheless, new functions were continually being added to batch processing, so that new programming techniques were required to keep it from spilling over into normal working hours. At present (Hillyer, 1984), AAS is being reorganized under pressure for further expansion and diversification. The differentiation of the "front and back ends" is continuing, as each of these major components is being given its own independent operating system.

Long-term memory structure is taking on a more associative configuration intended to reduce the redundancy created by the simpler organization of the old system. The relation between the complementary waking and dreaming cycles of AAS continues to evolve through an empirical process in which practical needs determine changes in design.

The similarities between batch processing in AAS and human dreaming do not seem to be accidental, then, but imposed by the nature of the information processing task they both address. In the same way, the eye of the octopus and the human eye are alike, despite their dissimilar origins. Under the pressure of natural selection, various arrangements of lens and screen have emerged to register visual imagery, but all are constructed according to the same principles of optics.

A sufficiently large information processing system must be constrained by similar general principles. New information taken in while the system is interacting with the outside world cannot be integrated immediately into long-term memory. Efficient distribution of new information into the internal organization of the system must be postponed until the system has been withdrawn from direct interaction with its environment, into a timeless state in which present and past can coexist. Reorganizing the memory structure while the system is interacting with the real world is like trying to build a boat while sailing in it.

The differences in scale between human dreaming and the nocturnal batch processing of AAS are instructive. The fact that AAS requires so many different housekeeping functions to do its simple version of dreaming suggests that humans must require many magnitudes more. The use of the sensory projection mechanisms in human dreaming for matching large and complicated blocks of current and past experience can only be a late refinement that organizes and integrates an enormous number of simpler functions like those employed by AAS.

The subjective experience of dreaming in humans can be seen as a late refinement in the evolution of an information processing technique employed since the earliest appearance of organisms able to learn from their interaction with the outside world. Large computer information systems are not only able to dream in this more primitive sense, but appear to be constrained to do so by the nature of their information processing tasks. The subjective experience of dreaming separates us from simpler systems like AAS, but we should be cautious about accepting definitions of mental functioning based on what distinguishes us from our evolutionary precursors rather than what links us with them.

DREAM INTERPRETATION

Traditional psychoanalytic dream theory explains the bizarre and idiosyncratic aspect of the dream as a cognitive breakdown resulting from the violent collision of drives and defenses, rather than as a specialized adaptive procedure for the matching of present experience with related events stored in long-term memory. This emphasis tends to discourage the analyst from taking full advantage of the information content of the dream reports he hears from his patients.

When the unusual subjective experience of the dream is seen in terms of its function within the highly evolved human information processing system, the role of dreaming and dream interpretation in clinical psychoanalysis takes on a new clarity. The dream becomes an integral part of the dreamer's mental life, central, in fact, to the process through which new internal structure is built from the materials of daily experience.

The initial goal of the interpreter is to disentangle this central function of dreaming from the obscurity caused by defensive displacements when affectively charged material is being processed. The familiar psychoanalytic method of dream interpretation was designed to circumvent these displacements. By tracing out the associative threads leading from each element of the dream, the analyst is often able to identify the dreamer's hidden motivational sources.

But this is only half the work of interpretation. Further on is the question of how the dreamer's conflicting motives in the present are clarified by the relation presented in the dream to earlier events in which he has attempted to resolve similar conflicts. The interpreter can often discover, through the dreamer's spontaneous associations and through tactful inquiries where necessary, the present and past events whose representations have been superimposed or condensed to form the composite imagery of the dream (Palombo, 1984b, in press).

He is then in a position to explore with the dreamer how his current wishes have been unconsciously identified with related wishes experienced and recorded in the past. The meaning of the dream lies in this series of identifications, rather than in any individual wish or impulse whose expression is represented in the dream or the dreamer's associations. The discovery of these identifications is not simply a matter of translating or decoding, but a creative act initiated in the process of dream construction itself and carried to completion in the analytic session.

In two recent papers (Palombo, 1983, 1984a), I have discussed how dream material serves as the source of structural continuity between the present and past in works of literature. The dream has this function in analytic interpretations as well. The dreamlike nocturnal procedures of computer systems like AAS cannot as yet participate in creative work in the way that human dreaming does. But the matching and organizational functions of the homely batch processing carried out every night by AAS are necessary prerequisites for the more surprising associative leaps of the human dreamer, the artist, or the psychoanalyst.

Dreaming is a synthetic activity of the mind, complementary in its scope to the logical and narrative modalities of waking thought. The creative power of human dreaming is one of the unique capacities of the human mind. But the process of dream construction itself is the evolutionary development of a simpler activity, an activity essential to every system that updates and extends its own inner organizational structure while interacting with the changing realities of the surrounding physical world.

REFERENCES

Aserinsky, E., & N. Kleitman (1953). Regularly occurring periods of eye motility and concomitant phenomena during sleep. *Science, 188,* 273–274.

Bjerre, P. (1936). *Das Traumen als Heilungsweg der Seele,* Zurich: Rascher Verlag.

Boden, M. (1977). *Artificial intelligence and natural man.* New York: Basic Books.

Breger, L. (1967). Function of dreams. Journal of *Abnormal Psychology Monograph. 72,* 1–27.

Dement, W. (1955). Dream recall and eye movements during sleep in schizophrenics and normals, Journal of *Nervous Mental Disease, 122,* 263–269.

Dement, W., & Wolpert, E. (1958). Relation of eye movement, body motility, and external stimulation to dream content, *Journal Experimental Psychology, 55,* 543–553.

Dennett, D. C. (1978). *Brainstorms*. Montgomery, Vt: Bradford Books.

Dewan, E. (1967). The programming (P) hypothesis for REM sleep, Air Force Cambridge Research Laboratories, Physical Science Papers, No. 338. Also *International Psychiatry Clinics*, 1970, *70*, 296–307.

Evans, C., & Newman, E. A. (1964). Dreaming: An analogy from computers. *New Scientist, 24*, 577–579.

Fishbein, W., (Ed.). (1981). *Sleep, dreams and memory*. Jamaica, NY: Spectrum Publications.

Freud, S. (1900). *The interpretation of dreams. Standard Edition* (Vols. 4 & 5). London: Hogarth Press, 1953.

Freud, S. (1917). *Introductory lectures on psychoanalysis.* Standard Edition, Vol. 15. London: Hogarth Press, 1955.

Greenberg, R., & Leiderman, P. H. (1966). Perceptions, the dream process and memory. An up-to-date version of 'Notes on a mystic writing pad.' *Comprehensive Psychiatry. 7*, 517–523.

Hawkins, D. (1966). A review of psychoanalytic dream theory in the light of recent psycho-physiological studies of sleep and dreaming, *British Journal of Medical Psychology. 39*, 85–104.

Hillyer, P. (1984). Out from under. *Think. 50*, 10–15.

Lindsay, P. H., & Norman, D. A. (1977). *Human information processing* (2nd ed.). New York: Academic Press.

Lowy, S. (1942). *Psychological and biological foundations of dream interpretation*, London: Kegan Paul, Trench, Trubner.

Palombo, S. R. (1976). The dream and the memory cycle, *International Review of Psycho-analysis. 3*, 65–83.

Palombo, S. R. (1978). *Dreaming and memory: A new information-processing model*. New York: Basic Books.

Palombo, S. R. (1980). The cognitive act in dream construction. *Journal of American Academy of Psychoanalysis, 8*, 186–201.

Palombo, S. R. (1983). The genius of the dream. *American Journal of Psychoanalysis, 43*, 301–313.

Palombo, S. R. (1984a). The poet as dreamer. *Journal of American Academy of Psychoanalysis, 12*, 59–74.

Palombo, S. R. (1984b). Deconstructing the manifest dream. *Journal of American Psychoanalytic Association, 32*, 405–420.

Palombo, S. R. (in press). Recovery of early memories associated with reported dreams, *American Journal of Psychiatry*.

Robert, W. (1886). *Der Traum als Naturnotwendigkeit Erklart*. Hamburg.

Scrima, L. (1982). Isolated REM sleep facilitates recall of complex associative information. *Psychophysiology, 19,* 252–259.

Simon, H. A. (1981). *The sciences of the artificial*. (2nd ed.). Cambridge, Mass: M.I.T. Press.

Sowa, J. F. (1984). *Conceptual structures: Information processing in mind and machine*. Reading, Mass: Addison-Wesley.

Wimbrow, J. H. (1971). A large-scale interactive administrative system, *IBM Systems Journal, 10,* 260–282.

CHAPTER 4

COLLABORATIVE DREAM INTERPRETATION[1]

Walter Bonime, M.D.

An explosive young college woman dreamt about eggs, some of which were bombs. We never precisely understood the eggs and bombs, but through a long, painful, increasingly intimate psychoanalytic struggle she was able to overcome her unhappy, self-destructive way of life.

DREAM WORK AND PSYCHOANALYTIC COLLABORATION

Collaboration is of the essence in the psychoanalytic process. It is clinically basic for optimal work with dreams. Quite apart from resulting insights, working with dreams itself contributes intrinsically to the psychoanalytic process. A contribution of immense value is in the psychotherapeutic engagement of patients (Bonime, 1969). Work with dreams often serves as an induction of the patient into

[1]This paper was previously published in the *Journal of the American Academy of Psychoanalysis,* Volume 14, No. 1, pages 15–26, January 1986.

analysis, into the most intense, sometimes almost new experience, of participating in an intimate cooperative activity.

Dealing with dreams helps as an induction into the clinical experience partly in an educational way. It is an excellent learning situation for free association. The abnormal imagery in dreams, the unnatural or unusual physical properties of live or inanimate objects, the altered appearance and character of people, the time and space distortions, all create a more consonant context for revealing the "meaningless" tangential associative fragments that are excluded from ordinary discourse. Reporting the dream sets a tone that tends to ease communicating what is awkwardly personal and seemingly irrational. Associative activity, risked with dream material, can serve as initiation and practical experience for free association in connection with accounts of waking life, including the therapeutic interpersonal relationship.

Psychoanalysis as a *necessarily* cooperative undertaking is a novel concept for the patient. The analyst can seriously convey that: "I don't know what your dream means and you don't know what your dream means, but we can work on it together. There's a fair chance we'll discover or better understand something about you that isn't now apparent to you or to me. We both become engaged in associative acitivity. I may see connections of an association of yours with something you've told me about yourself earlier. I may get a clue about something in your dream by recalling a personal life experience or something in a movie, a play, a book, or another person's life. My linkages may sound way off the mark to you, but at the same time trigger an illuminating thought or memory of your own." All this is the kind of comment one can make early in therapy and repeatedly in varying contexts. The example is condensed here. But it suggests the sense of mutual involvement that gradually replaces the patient's idea of "treatment" as something that another person does to you or for you.

Another cardinal area for collaboration in therapy is that of a person's feelings. Maximum clarity about affect is crucial for analysis. Exploration for and examination of emotions emphasize the requirement of working together. For the patient this concerns the detection, delineation, and communication of emotion. One often has to ask the patient what are or were his feelings connected with various experiences or moments of a particular happening or dream. It is possible for the analyst to observe a blush or a pallor or beads of perspiration, to hear a rumbling belly, to watch a hand become a fist—all of which signal some emotional turbulence. These signs, however, indicate only the existence of a tension, not its nature. A clenched fist can indicate not anger but taking courage. It could reflect endurance of physical or emotional pain. We need to inquire of the patient for the feeling. As analysts, by ourselves we can only speculate about the patient's affect. By ourselves we cannot know. Much of the time patient and analyst through dialogue discover a connection among a current incident, a memory and an emotion. That information may lead to further new connections for either or both participants. In addition, the joint achievement of greater understanding becomes for both individuals a valuable increment of collaborative experience—and capacity.

Engaging the patient in the psychoanalytic process is involving him in an intense interpersonal event. Participation by the patient in such functioning contributes crucially to healthy personality change. And within the *total* collaborative analytic endeavor, a major aspect of the conjoint work is with dreams (Bonime, 1969; See index, "collaborative process," in Bonime, 1962, 1982).

EVALYN, THE "ARISTOCRAT"

In order to establish a clinical framework for the ideas that will be discussed, I shall sketchily describe a young patient to whom I here give the name Evalyn.

During her years of analysis anger appeared as a recurrent motif in dreams, feelings, activities, and fantasies. It was revealed implicitly and explicitly in many reported experiences, frequently occurring as the determinant of her behavior. Working together she and I explored her self-destructive, self-retarding, often grandiose, frequently vindictive way of life that engendered in her almost constant pain. "God," she said, "I hope I can change. I really poison myself to hurt and deprive others." On occasion, when she was in particularly low spirits and wanting to stay home alone while her parents went to the country for a weekend, she would go along with them to the country precisely so that they would have to observe her misery. In one session she recounted how "I called my mother to say I couldn't come for dinner tomorrow. My mother expressed disappointment and I felt myself getting furious— I don't know why—I resent her taking enjoyment from me when I'm trying so hard not to be enjoyable. I dislike her for having interest in me. It's an investment: she calls it loving—but I don't think that's what it is."

One day Evalyn entered my office with a calm but definite fury in her face. She slammed the door shut and said, "I could explode!" and told how a car backing out of a garage had crossed the sidewalk in front of her and how she had banged the car with her fist. She dreamt about a cousin's basket of eggs which were bombs and were part of a puzzle she had to figure out so they wouldn't explode. I asked her if her cousin was explosive and she replied, "Yes, very!" A few moments later she added, "I just thought of the feeling of exploding and the phrase: "Walk-

ing on eggs.'' One day when I offered an insightful suggestion she reported having an immediate fantasy of hurling a
bomb at my file.

An attractive, bright, unsmiling young woman, Evalyn first came to see me at the end of an academically slug-
gish college year and made arrangements to start analysis
after summer vacation and at the start of a year of employment. She had been professionally advised to take a year
off from school for therapy and a job. An angry, underachieving young aristocrat, she had experienced humiliation over having to struggle in the process of learning. A
probable paradigmatic source of her procrastinative, defiant academic lag was a repeated bit of maternal advice:
''My mother used to say, 'You've got to work to make
people like you. If you don't, nobody will like you.' I'd feel
a rage when she'd say that.''

She often spoke of exploding. Her basic sense of self
was rooted in anger. As a child she would shut herself in
her room and scream with rage. She dreamt and fantasied,
as already told, about bombs. In the first few weeks of
analysis she said, ''I think I always felt unloved because I
was dark and used to thank my lucky stars I didn't have
black hair. But then I couldn't have been *really* loved if my
mother's love centered on hair color . . .'' There was much
hatred toward her mother for so undervaluing her. Three
days after the comment on her mother's lack of genuine
love she verbalized her sense of a compensatory grandiosity, her ''aristocracy.'' She said, ''I think what makes me
act like a queen is my expectation and my angry demands
to be treated like a queen—to get $100 back from a $5 investment.'' However, a very different kind of transaction
quite regularly took place and intensified her anger, her
defiance, her vengeance, and her grandiosity. She ex-
claimed, ''I'm always doing things for approval, especially
from mother. I obliterate myself and hate her for it. The

same with others. I don't *have* to do those things that I do for approval.''

At the start of analysis she was trying to learn typing to qualify for employment. She said, ''I want a job—I *won't* practice typing.'' (My association was her $5 investment.) But she went on, saying, ''I'm angry!'' and became silent. I asked her what she was thinking and she replied she had no thoughts. After a voiceless minute she blurted, ''It's *defiance*—I like the feeling of defiance!'' She was furious also at her father, whose interest in her hardly ever got beyond, ''What did you do in school today?'' A chemistry professor, he was popular with students, protegés and colleagues, who came great distances to a dinner honoring him on retirement. His daughter could hardly bear the thought of attending the affair and when he stood to acknowledge the tributes, she had the fantasy of hurling a bomb at him.

Her academic aristocracy was clearly exposed in one session when she stated, ''To study is to be square. To study is to do the expected.'' Her expectation was to comprehend without effort. She repeated, ''I want to get $100 for a $5 investment.'' She described how she would stop studying ''at the point of confusion. I've had relatively little experience of enjoyment of effort.''

One of those days on which she entered the office in a fury, ''ready to explode'' after her mother had again told her how she had to act in order to be liked, she said, ''If I could devise some way of hurting my mother that would not hurt me, I'd do that.'' In reply, I suggested, ''Then you'd be able to go ahead and fulfill your constructive motivations, do more of what you want to do for yourself.''

''Yes, of course,'' she responded, and explained that because of her mother she lacked ''motivation.''

When I offered the possibility that ''lack of motivation'' is an expression of revenge and added what was practically a quotation from herself, ''your predominating motivation is to hurt your mother," she had an immediate reply. "Lack of motivation and revenge are the same— that's what I *mean* when I say, 'lack of motivation.' " And over the weekend she entered in her notebook: "I will at *all costs* prevent her from having a successful motherhood . . . I'll show you what a shitty kid you produced." She seriously contemplated departing from the aristocracy of her home and, with her ne'er-do-well boyfriend, settling in a western hippie commune.

SCRIMA'S CONTRIBUTIONS

This fragmentary tracing of a grossly underachieving, wretched, raging adolescent-and-young-adult woman is a background for two themes about dreams. The major focus is clinical collaboration in working with dreams. The secondary focus is a consideration of and speculative elaboration of the relationship of psychophysiological involvement in both the dreaming and the collaborating processes.

The psychophysiological aspects involve the work of Scrima (1984) on dreams and memory. By studying narcoleptics, who uniquely achieve dreaming at sleep onset, Scrima found that pre-dream complex information was significantly better integrated *during dream sleep* than during an equivalent period of the waking state.[2]

The rapid eye movement (REM) or dream state with this unusually high degree of information integration, as

[2]Considerable sleep-dream-memory research including psychodynamic observation and formulation has taken place during the past nearly 2 decades. Representative contributions are those of Breger (1967), Cartwright (1975), Dewan (1970), Fishbein (1981), Greenberg (1974, 1975), and Greiser et al. (1972). Scrima's contribution, significantly confirmatory of previous work, might be regarded as a vivid paradigm for the REM integrative function.

demonstrated by Scrima's work, is also broadly known as "paradoxical sleep." It is so named by its resemblance to the waking state: the electroencephalographic (EEG) tracing, the respiratory and pulse variations are close to those of the waking state. Major differences from waking are central nervous system extensive physiological disconnection from voluntary muscle activity and a large degree of disconnection from incoming sensory stimuli. It is my speculation that the dream itself, uncontaminated by the "noise" of sensory stimuli, might be regarded as a state of pure free association—a state in which some of the associations are creatively modified into symbols and metaphors, occurring in developmental storylike form having parts with shifts of sequence, setting, and activity which are frequently bizarre. As with all human experience, the quality of the dream is characterized also by *affect* that may be single, multiple, variant, contradictory, and of a wide or constant or altering intensity. Of crucial importance, the dream is furthermore engendered under conditions that, unlike waking, do not demand concentration on or attention to immediate mental, social, and physical behavior.

Scrima's (1984) report of his research ends with the following emphases. He concludes that "dream sleep reflects an ongoing active process . . . that integrates information, enables . . . ever-increasing facility to retrieve memories . . . and allows ever increasing comprehension of our seemingly infinitely complex environment and human condition . . ." (p. 216). These conclusions provide a point of departure for clinical consideration and the focus on collaboration.

Constituting the base for collaboration in the clinical setting are two sets of information: that of the patient and that of the therapist. Through communication, empathy, and memory the two people seek *as high a correlation as possible* of their respective information and speculations about the patient's experience (including affect) and what it may reflect about his personality.

MUTUAL ATTENTION

A basic requirement for collaboration in psychoanalysis, and for collaborative working with dreams, is the most continuous possible concentrated attention. Such attentiveness applies to patient and analyst. Illumination of the patient's personality engendered by a dream experience comes from those fragments of the dream experience recaptured in memory during the waking state. Retrieved memories of the dreaming experience induce recall of further life experiences and speculatively inform these with the context in which the dream is being considered and perhaps was evolved. The aroused associative memories may also inform with important nuances the retrieved dream pieces and even the basic structure of the dream experience.

One might say it this way: the fragments of dream experience have been drawn and creatively assembled out of total (lifelong) life experience, and in the waking state become mnemonically linked with further old and recent data and probably with some of the original memories drawn upon in generating the dream. During the psychoanalytic hour, concentration on seeming irrelevancies and trivia may be a great strain, the possible source of boredom and woolgathering. But analyst or patient can also return with commitment to the affect and to the direction from which the associative train started. This resumption of genuine associative activity may occur if there seems likely to have been a resistance-motivated abandonment of exploration. To reembark or to move unpromisingly ahead is a difficult choice to evaluate. Would one be resuming a significant associative course? Would one be opting for or supporting elusiveness?

The importance of persistent concentration by both patient and therapist is twofold. First, it makes available as large a common store of potentially relevant information as possible. Second, it taps the fullest potential for mutual stimulation, that is, for cognitive, mnemonic, and affective reciprocal triggering.

Communication is especially important on the part of the patient, to extend the analyst's store of information about the patient's life experience, including the current relationships and the immediate, momentary therapeutic interpersonal attitudes. In the course of the therapeutic communication and associated interpersonal experience, both the patient and analyst are engendering expanding living data bases concerning the patient's life and personality. The patient's new experiences, felt and reported and observed, become integrated in the memory store of each, although for each in an idiosyncratic way. In the course of this therapeutic work the patient's trust in and closeness to the analyst increase. The analyst's understanding, desire to help the patient, to increase the patient's fulfillment and gratification, grow, and there can develop an even affectionate concern for the patient.

EVALYN: FURTHER EXPLORATIONS

The angry young woman we have described developed a growing trust and one day brought in a dream in which a man stood close to her in an elevator. She spoke of his "pulling me closer to him with his leg, like an octopus. I'm terrified and fight desperately to get away."

Through the complexities of the dream and interpretive attempts she made no reference to me until I asked if in any way I appeared in the dream. She said she had had the thought that I was the man in the elevator who *"pushed"* her away. At first when I asked her if she felt I appeared in the dream, she responded, with a humorous inflection, "Wht do *you* think?" and chuckled at the therapeutic role reversal. That in itself, at this point, was an act of trust and lack of fear. The dream revealed terror of my closeness, inherent in which was the danger of her being "pushed away." The session revealed a trust and friendly playfulness as she dodged my question. She trusted me but took at least a caricatured refuge in a familiar, adversarial role—one of coping with rejection.

This young woman began to move toward a constructive life course. She investigated some postgraduate possibilities. She had a dream that we explored together and that suggested correlations and an illumination of a great deal of her explosiveness and her self-wasting. An almost lost segment of the dream reflected a new, constructive self-direction. By this time in her analysis we had reviewed and examined many angers related to many people, rages associated with thousands of experiences of frustration, contempt, vindictiveness, humiliation, cynicism toward and hatred of her parents, particularly her mother. We both had large stores (only fractional on my part) of memories, infinite potential associative references related to her narrations of angry reactions to family and others, to self-destructive behaviors and depressions.

One may reasonably speculate that on the basis of the dream research earlier referred to the analyst will have many integrations of information about patients from sessions of the day that will occur in next-night sleep or be triggered by new experiences and processed during dream sleep on many succeeding nights. The analyst's continuing circuitries occurring as well during the day (though often disregarded as well as proceeding in unawareness) may also resonate with stimuli from other patients, from readings, television, and numerous interpersonal experiences. Tauber and Green (1959) have written about therapeutic introduction of their own dreams involving their patients. At the time of the dream to follow, this young woman and I had integrated in our memories a great deal about her life, wit ι which to hypothesize toward the goal of understanding both her personality and her personality changes in progress.

This bright, aloof, wealthy young woman at first trusted no one and went through many unproductive sessions before she began to express herself with any degree of openness. Even later, she often candidly refused to say what was in her mind. She brought in a dream during her fourth year of analysis that seemed to start like a nightmare. For several years she had had a boyfriend who, though usually jobless and indigent, had personal charm and occasional periods of ambitious activity and was accepted by her parents as their daughter's lover. The patient did not respect or love him or enjoy him sexually, but admittedly hung on to him because his constancy protected her from the anxious humiliations of the dating game.

During analysis she had barely succeeded in completing her Bachelor's at a top ranking university. After 2 years in a commercial institution where she felt miserable about wasting her life, she made a tentative decision to shift directions. She quit her job and was struggling to prepare for graduate work, but felt threatened by the prospect of resuming serious study. She would be years behind her academic peers and she faced the likelihood of having to strive intensively to hold her ground, to move ahead without excelling. She was also reluctant to gratify her parents with a respectable career. Above all, she clung to a pathology, insight into which she experienced mostly intellectually. She recognized her compulsively self-retarding, subjectively sensed *aristocracy of idleness*. Her wealth had shielded her against many developmental material deprivations and nurtured her grandiose sense of superiority to the pathetic, contemptible strivings of others.

Her dream came while she was struggling with the contemplation of starting graduate work.

> *In her dream there had been an implied nuclear deposit over the city where she lived. There was a gray fallout all around. Nobody else knew that there was radiation enough to be fatal to everyone within 2 days. There was a bridge across a river to a town where everybody was having a gay time, "living it up," unaffected by the nuclear bombing. Her mother urged the patient and the boyfriend to get over to that town.*

An association came to me in connection with the mother's urging her to the unaffected town across the river. The patient had frequently speculated and complained that because of her mother's own lack of achievement she had never truly wanted Evalyn to be more than a happy child. In the analysis the patient had already long recognized that she had felt torn between two life courses. One was achieving success that she would hate to see gratify her mother. The other was enduring a wasted life in order to shame, frustrate, and sadden her mother. (On graduating from college she despised her mother's excitement and spoke of delivering the diploma "into her hot little hands.")

Innumerable experiences of my listening and storing memories about Evalyn formed the basis of an important association in me. In connection with the happy town across the river from the radioactive fallout, I recalled and

mentioned the hippie commune which Evalyn had seriously considered going to live in. The patient immediately
said she had had the same association. We both felt it implied that a commune existence would wound the upper
middle-class mother; and Evalyn felt it would be a fitting
punishment for her mother's mixture of exaggerated prais-
ing and the consequent stunting and infantilizing Evalyn
had suffered.

Associating to the nuclear bombing she said emphati-
cally and obscurely, "Being responsible for my life is a
threatening state to be in." Then she added, "I have to
come out on top all the time; I can't even approach trying
to be responsible." It appeared she was saying that com-
petitively it would be a defeat for her to submit to being an
adult without a certainty of preeminence.

I then suggested, "Perhaps you were depressed and in
your depressive fury you wiped out the adult environment
which demands your participation and responsibility." I
added after a moment, "Why would your going to the other
town be like going to a commune?"

In response she recalled for the first time another bit
of the dream, which indicated that it had not been utterly
dominated by destructiveness and gloom. Visibly and au-
dibly brightening, she said, "I just remembered that near
the end of the dream the skies cleared and the sun came out
and I had a good feeling." Her association to this was a
sudden recall of the electrical blackout of New York City,
which had engendered so much unexpected friendliness
among virtual and complete strangers.

There seemed at this point to be a possible meaning of
the dream. It was the implication of a profound ambivalence toward her situation—perhaps a sense that her depressive, destructive nuclear fallout appearing first as a
catastrophe (like the New York blackout) could end as a

clearing of the air and a brightening of her prospects. She did not, the dream suggested, really have to destroy the world that challenged her aristocracy. She might feel better joining the ordinary herd of humanity by a return to school and by struggling academically among younger and possibly brighter students.

This dream was not fully understood or experienced, but productive associative and interpretive activity were initiated, and together we carried forward our exploration of Evalyn's feelings, decisions, functional obstacles, and productive resources. She was active not only in creating and reporting the dream, but in working with it. It is this kind of trend toward the patient's increasing participation in the total psychoanalytic process that I feel has advanced the practice of psychoanalysis. The progress has come in large measure through the collaborative use of dreams.

Clinical advance is indicated in the individual case of this angry, isolated, refractory young woman. In the latter briefly reported dream, the identical association to the commune was significant of patient and analyst making similar circuitry within laboriously, increasingly correlated data bases. When this instance occurred, both of us were engaged in free association. The commune represented for both of us her wish to escape to a world of minimal responsibility. My own offer of an interpretive hunch was derived from my integrated memories of her, and perhaps, too, my feeling for her. Her hunch that her dream town was the commune not only demonstrated our consensual response to this idiosyncratic symbol, but increased the intensity of her search for the meaning in the dream. This effort resulted in additional recall of significant items obliterated from the original report: the clearing of the air and the sun coming out. Still further, accompanying these changes was another and extremely important affect, particularly important in connection with dimly formed plans for committing herself to a positive direction in life. With the air clearing and the sun coming out, she said, "I had a good feeling."

The focus on feelings, often insufficiently attended, brought to the surface the intensity of her depressive, radiating, nuclear fury. It also revealed, through the delayed recall of the clearing air and appearance of the sun, her reluctantly acknowledged experiential optimism about her new emerging academic direction in life. It, incidentally, demonstrated a close correlation of dream metaphor with waking affect and activity.

This dream also highlights the basically personal and idiosyncratic source of symbols. Interpretive activity with dream symbols is often disadvantageously confined to a somewhat standardized professional province. Much more clinically contributory is an open-ended mutual clinical exploration. The commune reflected not only Evalyn's desire to escape self-development and to increase the humiliation of her ambitious mother. It also helped to sharpen her concept of her mother's ambivalence toward her as expected to amount to something (to enhance the aristocratic myth of the family), but who should also remain childish and without a career so as never to excel over the mother.

Much of Evalyn's eventual trust in me, her willingness to express feeling, developed to a significant extent in the course of our joint exploration of initially totally inexplicable dream material. Speculatively, the more intensive a collaboration, the more intensive will be the associative attention and reporting. The attentiveness and communication stimulate reciprocally and both build a more accessible, more actively integrated store of memory. Collaboration is itself the development of both independence and trust within a complex interpersonal setting.

In all of this intensive, attentive role of the patient, the analyst himself becomes deeply influenced. The analyst's conception of the professional role becomes more humble as he, too, has been drawn into a more active, equal, and intimate collaboration with the patient. The hard work of concentration on all that is produced in the clinical setting leads to integration of great amounts of often unpredictably useful memory stores. A great deal of such data can be lost in spells of boredom and inattention. It is material that might otherwise yield significant clues to understanding, if captured and available for mnemonic reference and symbolic mutation. If attended, it could, in accordance with much clinical and laboratory study, be included in integration with "all our experience."

Finally, there is no longer *the* interpretation of a dream. There is, instead, a mutual interpretive process consisting of a risk-taking, ongoing, patient-analyst, collaboration. It involves a conscientious detection, delineation, and communication of affect and an interaction of associative and interpretive activities. I believe the results of a cooperative operational atmosphere in analysis are in the direction of greater usefulness and understanding of dreams, and greater personal growth for both patient and therapist.

REFERENCES

Bonime, W. (1969). The use of dreams in the therapeutic engagement of patients. *Contemporary Psychoanalysis 6*, 1, 13–30.

Bonime, W., with Bonime, F. (1962). *The clinical use of dreams.*

New York: Basic Books (1962–1982); New York: Da Capo Press New York (1982–).

Breger, L. (1967) Function of dreams. *Journal of Abnormal Psychology Monograph* No. 72, 1–28. (Whole Number: 641)

Cartwright, R. D., Lloyd, S., Butters, E., Weiner, L., McCarthy, L., & Hancock, J. (1975). Effects of REM time on what is recalled. *Psychophysiology 12*: 561–568.

Dewan, E. M. (1970). The programming (P) hypothesis for REM sleep. In E. Hartmann (Ed.), *Sleep and dreaming*, pp. 295–307. International Psychiatry Clinics, 7 (2), Boston: Little, Brown.

Fishbein, W. (1981). (Ed.). *Sleep, dreams and memory* (Part Two: Human Research). New York: Spectrum Publications.

Greenberg, R., & Pearlman, C. (1974). Cutting the REM nerve: An approach to the adaptive role of REM sleep. *Perspectives in Biology and Medicine*, Summer, 513–521.

Greenberg, R., & Pearlman, C. (1975). A psychoanalytic dream continuum: The source and function of dreams. *The International Review of Psychoanalysis, 2*, 4, 442–448.

Greiser, C., Greenberg, R., & Harrison, R. H. (1972). The adaptive function of sleep: The differential effects of sleep and dreaming on recall. *Journal of Abnormal Psychology, 80*, 3:280–286.

Scrima, L. (1984). Dream sleep and memory: New findings with diverse implications. *Integrative Psychiatry, 2*, 6, 211–216.

Tauber, E., & Green, M. (1959). *Prelogical experience*. New York: Basic Books.

CHAPTER 5

MANIFEST DREAM ANALYSIS IN CONTEMPORARY PRACTICE

Silas L. Warner, M.D.

This chapter is divided into three parts: The first part is a brief history up to the present of how the manifest dream has been understood and used in clinical practice. The second part contains the results of a survey from the current psychoanalytic literature as to how the manifest dream has been dealt with in actual case reports. The third part consists of four brief clinical vignettes from my own practice. Using this clinical material I shall demonstrate how certain dreams, with easily understood manifest content, can signal an important turning point in the therapeutic process.

THE MANIFEST DREAM IN CLINICAL PRACTICE: A RETROSPECTIVE

Freud first brought to our attention the relationship between the manifest and latent dream content in his 1900 seminal work, *The Interpretation of Dreams*. As to the relative importance of the manifest and latent dream content, Freud wrote, "Now that the application of our procedure for interpreting dreams enables us to disclose a latent content in them which is of far greater significance than their manifest one . . ." (p. 163).

Freud (1900) viewed the manifest dream as a conglomerate (p. 449) or a facade (1915–1917, p. 181). The order and form of the manifest dream was irrelevant according to Freud. In interpreting the dream it was first to be broken up into separate pieces, to each of which the dreamer was to free associate. Even after Freud changed his model of the mind from the topographical to the structural, he did not revise his dream theory accordingly. In his later writing (1940) he finally acknowledged that "dreams may arise either from the id or from the ego" (p. 166). He also made a distinction between the motivating factors for two basic categories of dreams, "dreams from above and dreams from below". The dreams from below were those arising from unconscious infantile strivings. The new category, the dreams from above, were derived from "thoughts or intentions of the day before" (1923, p. 111).

In 1901, Freud published a shortened version of *The Interpretation of Dreams* which he titled *On Dreams*. He divided dreams into three categories "in respect of the relation between their latent and manifest content" (p. 642). His first category was that of intelligible dreams where "the manifest and latent content coincide and there appears to be a consequent saving in dream-work" (p. 643). Unfortunately, Freud never elaborated on this category.

The next major effort to examine the manifest dream was by Erikson in 1954. He points out that, "unofficially, we often interpret dreams entirely or in parts on the basis of their manifest appearance. Officially, we hurry at every confrontation with a dream to crack its manifest appearance as if it were a useless shell and to hasten to discard this shell in favor of what seems to be the more worth-while core'' (p. 17). Erikson creates an ''outline of dream analysis,'' starting with an inventory of manifest dream configurations. Using Freud's *Irma* dream, Erikson carries out an exhaustive dream analysis and demonstrates the importance of the manifest dream content.

In 1969, Spanjaard summarized the literature on the manifest dream content. He theorized that ''the manifest dream content usually has a subjectively conflictual aspect, and that this aspect offers us the opportunity to evaluate the most superficial layer of the conflict and thus to arrive at a construction of the potentially most useful interpretation'' (p. 224).

In commenting on Freud's warning that the manifest dream content should not be taken seriously, Spanjaard notes that Freud ''often trespasses against this very rule'' (p. 224). For example, in the Irma manifest dream, Freud criticizes Irma for not having accepted his solution. This criticism by Freud then becomes an essential part of the dream interpretation.

Freud so dominated dream theory that only slowly did non-Freudian theories about dreams appear. One new developmental stream was created by those theorists who believed that dreams served adaptive functions, above and beyond Freud's cathartic function. They also dealt more directly with the manifest content of the dream.

Leon Saul (1972) was one of the first psychoanalysts who closely studied the manifest dream. He summarized his views as follows. ''The manifest dream exquisitely reveals the whole interplay of motivations. What of the id comes through and the form of distortion imposed by superego and ego are there evidenced for the discerning eye. It portrays the upshot, the solution for the ego, what the person is really like, what he wants, and what he will allow himself to do. In general, the daydream visualizes what a person wants consciously while the manifest dream during sleep represents what he permits himself to have."

Saul continues, ". . . the manifest dream is the best possible guide for making the interpretation itself. The manifest dream represents, as we have noted, a certain level of psychic activity—not libidinal level, but level of consciousness and of repression. It is deep enough to be unfallibly revealing and yet not so deep that the unconscious processes are unintelligible or unacceptable to the patient. The manifest dream tells with great accuracy the level or depth at which the interpretation should be made.

"The manifest dream is the product of many such deeper forces, but if these are dealt with simply as they appear, undue resistances are not mobilized. And the analysis proceeds in a smoother, faster fashion than it does if the analyst is not careful to follow the manifest dream as exactly as possible in making his interpretation to the patient. In most cases what the ego represents and accepts in the manifest dream it will accept in interpretation without being greatly disturbed; if the ego accepts and acts on an impulse in the dream, this it is close to being able to do so in waking life since the manifest dream is the form given the unconscious forces and material by the ego in order to make them more acceptable; it tells the form in which the interpretation will be more acceptable" (p. 221–222).

The sleep research laboratories of the 1950s and 1960s introduced the concept of rapid-eye-movement (REM) sleep. This led to the study of REM dreams. Greenberg and Pearlman concluded in 1975 that "REM sleep is involved in information processing in the service of emotional adaptation." They collected and examined dream material in the sleep laboratory during an ongoing psychoanalysis. They found "it important to learn the patient's dream language as shown by his manifest dreams. The manifest dream then provides a vivid subjective view of the patient's current adaptive tasks—an indication of what is active in the analysis." They concluded that "dreams portray the struggle, inherent in the interaction between the wishes of the past and the needs of the present, and reflect the process of integration which appears to take place in REM sleep" (p. 441).

Dr. Greenberg, besides being an expert in the sleep laboratory is also a psychoanalyst. In offering his new formulations in dream psychology and dream interpretation he does not use the traditional concepts of disguise and latent content. He explains (1985) these omissions as follows:

"To begin with, the evidence for drive discharge in dreams has not been confirmed by studies of REM sleep and REM deprivation. The idea of disguise derives from the notion that it is necessary to hide the meaning of the dream in order to conceal the forbidden drives that seek expression. Without the concept of drive discharge, the idea of disguise is no longer necessary. Latent content also assumes a hidden meaning for the dream. In line with this thinking, we find that the manifest content is not an indifferent daily residue which is the carrier of the latent dream wishes, but actually represents issues with which the dream is dealing. Understanding of the dream evolves from an understanding of the sources of manifest content. Thus, we are offering an alternative to the traditional approach to the dream and not just a negation of the classical theory and practice."

Another practicing psychoanalyst, Stanley R. Palombo (1978), has combined the traditional psychoanalytic model with a new information processing model to construct a revised dream theory. Palombo views dreaming as being part of the memory cycle. It is through this cycle that new experience is filed into appropriate associational locations in the brain's long-term memory bank. In dreams we automatically match present with past experience and filter through the salient information into permanent memory. Greenberg's understanding of the dream has many similarities to Palombo's. There are also some significant differences that are beyond the scope of this paper. Suffice it to say that both Greenberg and Palombo have combined a clinical psychoanlytic approach with sleep-lab REM-NREM studies that provide us with a much better understanding of the manifest and latent dream content. Their work also links the dream's manifest content to the dreamer's current conflict and the day's residue.

Another psychoanalyst who has given us a new viewpoint on the manifest dream is the late Heinz Kohut. In developing his self-psychology (1977) he described dreams from patients whom he diagnosed as having narcissistic personality disorders. These dreams were called "self-state dreams". They are characterized by the fact that "free associations do not lead to unconscious hidden layers of the mind, at best they provide us with further imagery which remains on the same level as the manifest content of the dream. The scrutiny of the manifest content of the dream and of the associative elaborations of the manifest content will then allow us to recognize that the healthy sectors of the patient's psyche are reacting with anxiety to a disturbing change in the condition of the self—manic overstimulation, or a serious depressive drop in self-esteem, or to the threat of the dissolution of the self" (p. 109–110). Kohut found such "self-state dreams" to be similar to the dreams of children, or to the dreams of a traumatic neurosis, or to dreams found in toxic states.

TREATMENT OF THE MANIFEST DREAM
IN CASE STUDIES: A SURVEY

I was struck by Erickson's (1954) statement that, "unofficially, we often interpret dreams entirely or in part on the basis of their manifest appearance. Officially, we hurry at every confrontation with a dream to crack its manifest appearance as if it were a useless shell and to hasten to discard this shell in favor of what seems to be the more worthwhile core" (p. 17). It has been my impression that contempory analysts are making use of the dream's manifest content much more frequently today than in previous years.

I decided to do a survey of four psychoanalytic journals from the start of 1984 to November 1985. I looked for dreams reported in clinical case descriptions and compared the use of the manifest and latent dream contents in the dream interpretations. I arbitrarily chose the *International Journal of Psychoanalysis,* the *Journal of the American Psychoanalytic Association,* the *Journal of the American Academy of Psychoanalysis,* and the *Psychoanalytic Quarterly.* I located some 25 editions of these journals during this period with almost 60 clinical reports of dreaming. I made a tripartite division between the two extremes: dream interpretations from mainly manifest content, and those from mainly latent content. In the middle are those dream interpretations which use both manifest and latent dream content equally. The classical Freudian analyst would make his dream interpretation from mainly latent dream content. My results are shown below:

1. *International Journal of Psychoanalysis*
   20 dreams— 4 mostly manifest
               15 both manifest and latent
               1 mostly latent
2. *Psychoanalytic Quarterly*
   12 dreams—5 mostly manifest
              6 both manifest and latent
              1 mostly latent

3. *Journal of the American Academy of Psychoanalysis*
   10 dreams—8 mostly manifest
   2 both manifest and latent
4. *Journal of the American Psychoanalytic Association*
   15 dreams—6 mostly manifest
   9 both manifest and latent

Out of 57 dreams the manifest dream content was used mainly for interpretations in 23 instances, and partly in 32. This means that in 55 out of 57 dreams there was from approximately 50 percent up to 100 percent use of the manifest dream. In only 2 dreams was the dream interpretation made mainly from the latent content, as Freud had suggested.

This confirms Erikson's hunch that even the classical analysts are using the manifest dream content extensively in their dream interpretation in the mid-1980s. I realize that the case reports in the journals were condensed and may not have included as many free associations as actually occurred. However, again and again the analyst is guided by the clear meaning of the manifest content which then becomes an integral part of the dream interpretation.

It is instructive to compare the change in attitude of panel discussions from the American Psychoanalytic Association meetings in 1956 and in 1984. Sterba made the following concluding remark denigrating the manifest dream in 1956, "real dream interpretation from the manifest content alone was no more possible than an attempt to read a letter from its envelope without opening it" (p. 137).

In 1984 the panel report concluded that, "on the basis of the panelists' presentations we must award the manifest dream, a favored, but not unique place in clinical work" (p. 161).

FOUR CLINICAL VIGNETTES

I believe that certain patients consistently produce dreams in which clear meaning can be found in the manifest content. The manifest content theme usually can be further confirmed by the latent dream content and the day residue. In a previous article (1983) I demonstrated that "successful" manifest dreams in certain patients parallel their clinical improvement. I intend to describe how certain patients (names are fictitious) show "turning point dreams" (TPDs) that clearly illustrate the attainment of certain therapeutic landmarks.

For example, I consider it a TPD when the analyst first clearly appears in a patient's dream as a helping or comforting figure. This is evidence that the patient has internalized the analyst as an image within his psyche. An illustration of this is Peggy's dream in her third month of psychotherapy.

"I am in a room which looks like the living room of our old house. There is a family gathering; it looks like either Thanksgiving or Christmas. An older man with gray hair is sitting in a red stuffed chair near the fireplace. He smiles at me and I go sit on his lap and put my head on his shoulder. I feel very warm and comfortable."

Peggy smiled at me sitting in my office red chair and said, "we both know that you are the gray-haired man." Her further associations confirmed this interpretation, as well as her current good feelings. Prior to this dream, she had felt alone and needy, having just broken off a long-term relationship. Her father had been ill and inattentive during most of her life. Her mother was more caring but remained absorbed by her own career. Peggy had always felt emotionally deprived.

This TPD showed that Peggy had admitted me into her

mind's inner sanctum and a positive transference was being established. Soon Peggy started to idealize me and demand more time and attention. When she didn't rapidly become my most important patient, she became angry and brooded. She is just now beginning to lessen her demands on me and externalize some of her needs to others. At twenty-eight years of age, she is finally showing an improved self-esteem and is no longer depressed.

The next vignette concerns Marcia who was seventy-four years old when I saw her. She had grown children and several grandchildren, but was still young and romantic at heart. I had seen her for about 3 years in psychotherapy when she was in her early fifties. She was then unhappily married and depressed. She worked through her feelings of anger and disappointment at her husband and returned to her nursing career. She felt reasonably well at that point and terminated psychotherapy. Subsequently, her first husband died. She felt some of her depression returning and considered resuming psychotherapy. However, it was not until she met a young man in his late twenties and began to feel romantically involved that she finally called me. She knew that in this relationship she was living out a childhood fantasy, but she could not break it off. She felt addicted to Hank, even though she knew that he was irresponsible and unreliable. Marcia had just had a cataract operation, but could feel young again in Hank's presence. She could not be seen with Hank in public and could not tell her children of the relationship. In our first interview, she told me her story and urged me not to think badly of her.

In the second interview, she related the following dream from the previous night.

"I was in an unknown building looking for the ladies' room. I find it and go in. I pull my skirt up and my underwear down and urinate on the floor. Another women comes in and asks me if I know anything about the puddle on the floor. I reply that I had not noticed it and had no idea how it got there. I then wake up but soon fall back to sleep with the same dream. This time the ending was different. I now admit that I was responsible for the puddle on the floor."

Marcia looked up at me and said, "I don't even have to associate to that dream. It is clearly a dream of defiance and guilt. My conscience is telling me that I should no longer see Hank. It is not proper for a seventy-four year-old grandmother to have a twenty-eight-year-old gigolo as her lover and companion. But I've grown tired of always conforming and never doing what I really wanted to and so now I am telling the establishment to go screw itself. I don't sound like a lady when I talk this way but I have a lifetime of resentment which constantly fuels my defiance. I was raised to be very sensitive to what others thought of me and to try to please everybody. I got so good at it that I started to think that this cheerful, selfless woman who was always most interested in other people and their needs was the real me. Part of me recognizes that this was a facade and that sooner or later I would be exposed for what I really was. In the dream, I deny my defiant wrongdoing at first, but my conscience is so strong that I finally confess it."

In Marcia's dream, where the manifest content is clear and fits in with the current conflict, I don't believe it is necessary to dissect out the infantile roots. In fact, the infantile roots are expressed in the overt conflict that so clearly comes out in the manifest content of the dream. It is a metaphor concerned with a lifelong tendency towards submissiveness, coupled with a lifelong resentment of such submissiveness and a strong desire to be defiant towards authority. Since this pattern is so clearly illustrated in the manifest content, it seems redundant to elaborate on the theme by attempting to find associations connected to childhood. What difference would it make if Marcia remembered a childhood scene about wetting her bed and incurring her parents' wrath? At best, it could only help to convince her that this is a recurrent theme that has been present throughout her life. But she has already acknowledged that this conflict between submissiveness, defiance, and guilt is very familiar to her. The other area that was explored in this dream was how it articulated with her transference feelings. She anticipated this by telling me that in returning to see me after all these years, she felt like a naughty little girl dutifully confessing to her father who was a strong authority figure. Intellectually, she knew that I would not be sitting in judgment on her, but emotionally she experienced me as she did her father and older brothers. We all wanted her to submit to our will and to be a good girl. She wanted to thumb her nose at us all, and tell us that she was a grown adult and could do as she pleased. When I did not criticize her for becoming involved with a young man 50 years her junior, she felt relieved and understood. We were then able to explore all sides of her conflict to help her to resolve it. My nonjudgmental approach to her conflict was a corrective emotional experience for Marcia.

Bill, a single, forty-four-year-old lawyer, entered analysis 1 year after his mother's death. He had experienced feelings of unreality along with symptoms of depersonalization and depression. He knew that these feelings began after his mother's death, and that he had not resolved his feelings about her. We thoroughly explored his feelings towards both his mother and father. He knew that his mother was overprotective, and said that it was not until he was forty years of age that he was able to leave home. Now he felt guilty because his father was living alone and had pleaded with Bill to return home. He was angry at his mother for leaving him in such a mess. He was aware that he had mixed feelings towards his mother; he missed her and felt close to her, but he was also glad to have escaped from her clutches. He also felt guilty that he had been out of the country when she suddenly died. In his second year of analysis, he had the following dream:

"I was in the hospital with my mother who was dying. Her face looks very peaceful. I tuck in the covers around her shoulders. I tell her that I love her and ask her to nod if she understands me. She nods and smiles. I tell her again and she nods and smiles some more. Her eyes are then tightly closed and I feel calm and peaceful."

This dream was a TPD for Bill. He was able to work through his guilt towards his mother by dreaming that he was with her, comforting her at the end. He had always intended to have played this role with her. He had also resolved his feelings towards his father by arranging for him to live in a nearby retirement village along with many of his friends. Bill did have some associations to this dream, but they did not add to the central dynamics that showed so clearly in the dream's manifest content. There were other issues that we worked on subsequently in the analysis. However, resolving his ambivalent feelings towards his mother remained central.

Betty was originally referred to me when she was forty-five years old. She was living alone in the house where her father had died 10 years ago and her mother 3 years ago. She was single and had a career teaching the piano to children. In her loneliness she had turned towards the Catholic church and attended mass daily. She became attached to her parish priest and began to notice how he seemed to direct whatever he said at her. Her family physician told her that she was having ideas of reference and should see a psychiatrist. By a quirk of fate my office was not far from her church and so she decided to see another psychoanalyst, Dr. Adams. She had a very good therapeutic experience with him after having developed a positive transference. After 4 years he told her that he was moving his practice several hundred miles away and could no longer see her. Unfortunately, he only allowed her 2 months to resolve this positive transference and to start working with another psychoanalyst. She was crushed and angry at his imminent departure, and developed more ideas of reference. At first, she refused to see anyone else. She finally agreed to see Dr. Barnes, whose office was in the same suite as that of Dr. Adams.

From the start, her work with Dr. Barnes was a disaster. He received all the negative feelings that Dr. Adams had been spared. She claimed that he did not understand her and that he was greatly inferior to Dr. Adams. When he interpreted this as negative transference derived from her relationship to her father, Betty scornfully rejected his interpretation. She accused Dr. Barnes of being a selfish narcissist who showed no empathy for her. After a year of analysis she reported a dream to him in which she walked into his office, pulled a gun out of her purse and shot him. Dr. Barnes became very alarmed by this dream and referred her for a consultation with his own analyst. He advised Betty to see another analyst. Much to Dr. Barnes's relief she accepted this recommendation. By this time I had moved my office from proximity to her Catholic church and she came to see me.

I knew that I should not let her transference feelings become too intense if I were to help her. I used a Kohutian approach with her, trying to be optimally empathetic and validating her perceptions when appropriate. Her main complaint about me was that I was "too neutral" and that our sessions did not generate the strong feelings she had with both Dr. Adams and Dr. Barnes. We discussed realistically the reasons for this. Her self-concept improved and she started to socialize more. After about 3 years we agreed to set a termination date. She then brought in a dream that she said was her first dream with Dr. Adams.

"I am crossing a bridge wearing a lovely pink chiffon dress. I felt very pretty and I reached the other side of the bridge. There I saw my mother sitting hunched over, bloody, wounded, and near death. I approached her but then I abruptly turned around and went back over the bridge. I noticed some blood on my dress. On the other side of the bridge I saw my father dressed in a black suit. He looked like a mortician. He was reading a newspaper and I went over to him and tugged at his arm. I wanted to be close and talk to him. He motioned at me with his hand and pointed to a nearby limousine. I looked at the limousine and saw a man sitting in it wearing a red and white cassock. He was a Catholic prelate, probably a bishop or monsignor. I got into the car and we drove off."

Betty explained that Dr. Adams had interpreted this dream as having been a review of her life. She viewed her mother as having been badly hurt and wounded by life itself and by her father. She refused to follow in her mother's footsteps and instead sought solace and closeness with her father. He rejected her and sent her to be taken care of by the Catholic prelate. Her sexuality was denied and transcended by a spiritual commitment. Betty said that in her analysis with Dr. Adams she had achieved both caring and acceptance by a father substitute. She added that if only he had remained in this area she would have been fine. I asked her if she had any new associations to the dream. She replied that she only had one. She was reminded by the dream of watching a TV news report that showed vice-presidential candidate Geraldine Ferraro crossing a bridge, waving to the voters in an open limousine. I asked her to associate to Geraldine Ferraro. Betty replied that she strongly disliked her, because she represented all the things that Betty could have been and never was. They both came from working-class uneducated parents. Ferraro became well educated, successful politically, married, had children, and became affluent. These were all things that Betty had wanted but that her fears and inhibitions kept her from realizing.

We reviewed her dependency patterns, her trouble breaking away from her mother and her failure to form a close relationship with a man; how she, in fantasy, became dependent on a Catholic priest and then developed ideas of reference towards him. This was transferred to her relationship with Dr. Adams whom she had placed on a pedestal. We agreed tht the Catholic prelate with whom she went off in a limousine represented Dr. Adams who would lead her into the promised land. I asked her how she thought I might fit into this picture and she said that I reminded her of George Bush. When Ferraro and Bush debated she was struck by my resemblance to George Bush. She noticed how Geraldine Ferraro got the best of him. She "set him up" and he hurt his own image by being so patronizing to her. This reminded her of how I, at times, seemed like a professor who was lecturing to her.

In the last month before termination we reviewed her life and her unrealized aspirations. She had believed that she had to be a superstar like Geraldine Ferraro and always impress other people. She was now better able to accept herself, and felt more relaxed and friendly around people. After lessening her efforts to impress others she became less hostile and critical. She now appreciated her creative mind, good sense of humor, and good health. She began genuinely to enjoy teaching the piano to children, and viewed it as a worthy career rather than a second-rate job.

I have presented two of Betty's dreams, both of which could be readily understood from knowing her basic dynamics, current life, and transference situations. The dream about shooting Dr. Barnes was obviously a product of her frustration and negative transference feelings towards him. Such directly expressed hate and violence would be very threatening to most analysts. His constant struggle with her negative feelings seemed insoluble and his decision to have her seen in consultation was very prudent.

Her initial dream with Dr. Adams was a review of her pre-analytic life and her fantasies about what would happen to her in analysis. It also served us as a pretermination dream. It brought together material that we had discussed many times. It also provided a very valuable association, her identification with Geraldine Ferraro and seeing me as George Bush. This further confirmed our previous analytic work, and it provided for us a new metaphor expressing the transference, making it even more authentic for Betty. I might have flushed out many more associations to this dream, but I felt they would only muddy the waters. It was more important to focus on the central issues and prepare to terminate. I believe this demonstrates an initial dream becoming a turning point dream (TPD) that validated Betty's readiness for termination.

DISCUSSION

Most of us still can clearly recall our sense of awe when we first read Freud's *Interpretation of Dreams*. Suddenly we were transfixed by a glimpse into a new and marvelous world. The thoroughness and brillance of this seminal work reveals Freud's genius. His understanding of dreams was so conclusive that it seemed impossible that any changes would ever have to be made. A few brave individuals have tried to modify his dream theory, often resulting in their excommunication from the Freudian establishment. Freud's loyal followers developed such an intense narcissistic investment in his paradigms that attempts at modification were virtually forbidden (Rothstein, 1980). The natural evolution of psychoanalytic theory was thereby blocked. This has been especially true in the resistance to changing the position of the manifest dream. Freud initially took a strong stand against attributing too much importance to the manifest dream. Only grudgingly did Freud pay more attention to the manifest dream when he changed from the topographical to the structural model of the mind. Finally, in 1954, Erikson reminded analysts that unofficially we all make use of the manifest dream in our dream interpretations.

As an analogy, I remember playing baseball as a boy. We were taught that you must catch the baseball with two hands. Today all baseball players catch a baseball with one hand. This is similar to using the manifest dream in a dream interpretation. The baseball glove is improved, the players are better conditioned and more knowledgeable. Psychoanalytic theory is improved and our techniques are much better. Using the manifest dream skillfully increases our efficiency without sacrificing accuracy. Nevertheless, we must still continue to obtain associations and integrate our interpretations with the latent dream content as well.

Psychoanalysts and psychotherapists are currently being forced to think carefully about the number of psychotherapy sessions. Most insurance companies are now

limiting the number of sessions. Like golf players, psychotherapists will now have to do their job more efficiently
with the fewest strokes (or fewest interviews). One key to
this is taking advantage of what the manifest dream offers.
It provides a model of how the patient's ego is responding
to conflicts and adapting. The current success of short-term
dynamic psychotherapy illustrates how, within a limited
time, patients can be greatly helped. Because of economic
pressure all psychotherapists will be forced to work more
efficiently while still retaining their therapeutic skills. This
will provide a challenge to all of us, and should motivate
us to use the manifest dream effectively.

SUMMARY AND PROSPECT

The use of the manifest dream in contemporary psychoanalytic practice has been discussed. Originally, Freud
ignored the manifest dream and focused on the latent dream
content. More recently, analysts have increased their use
of the manifest dream in making a dream interpretation.

In this chapter I have reported on a survey of the reported dreams in four psychoanalytic journals over the past
2 years. These dreams were studied as to the relative use
of the manifest and latent content in making a dream interpretation. The results clearly show that contemporary analysts are using the manifest dream much more than they
did in the past.

Finally, I presented four case vignettes. Each one had
a special dream whose manifest content clearly showed that
a therapeutic milestone had been reached. I called this
special type of dream a turning point dream (TPD).

The advantages of focusing more on the manifest

dream content were then discussed. Current insurance coverage often limits the number of psychotherapy sessions. This should motivate the therapist to use each session as efficiently as possible. I believe that effective use of the manifest dream can improve therapeutic efficiency. Perhaps Freud's well-known dictum can now be changed to, "the manifest dream is the royal road to the unconscious."

BIBLIOGRAPHY

Erikson, E. H. (1954). The dream specimen of psychoanalysis. *Journal of American Psychoanalytic Association, 2.*
Freud, S. (1900). The interpretation of dreams. Standard Edition (Vols. IV and V). London: The Hogarth Press, 1953.
Freud, S. (1901). On dreams. Standard Edition (Vol. 5). London: Hogarth Press, 1953.
Freud, S. (1915–1917). Introductory lectures on psychoanalysis. Standard Edition, Vol. 15.
Freud, S. (1923). Remarks on the theory and praxis of dream interpretation. Standard Edition (Vol. 19).
Freud, S. (1940). An outline of psychoanalysis. Standard Edition (Vol. 23).
Greenberg, R. (1985). The dream problem and problems in dreams. From *Dreams: New Frontiers* Symposium, Philadelphia, Mar. 1985.
Greenberg, R., & Pearlman, C. (1975). A psychoanalytic dream continuum: The source and function of dreams. *International Review of Psychoanalysis, 2.*
Kohut, H. (1977). The restoration of the self. New York: International Universities Press.
Palombo, S. (1978). Dreaming and memory, A new information-processing model. New York: Basic Books.
Panel report. (1956). The dream in the practice of psychoanalysis. *Journal of American Psychoanalytic Association, 4.*

Panel report by Pulver, S., & Renik, I. (1984). The clinical use of the manifest dream. *Journal of American Psychoanalytic Association, 32.*

Rothstein, A. (1980). Psychoanalytic paradigms and their narcissistic investment. *Journal American Psychoanalytic Association,* Vol. 28, #2.

Saul, L. J. (1972). Psychodynamically based psychotherapy. New York: Science House.

Spanjaard, J. (1969). The manifest dream content and its significance for the interpretation of dreams. *International Journal of Psychoanalysis, 50.*

Warner, S. (1983). Can psychoanalytic treatment change dreams? *Journal American Academy of Psychoanalysis,* Vol. 11.

CHAPTER 6

THE DREAM REVISITED

Some Changed Ideas Based on a
Group Approach

Montague Ullman, M. D.

Since the mid-1970s I have been working with dreams
and teaching therapists about dreams in a way that is quite
different in its format from the way the practice and teaching of dreams is usually structured. The small group process I use originated as a teaching instrument but I found
it equally useful in extending dream work into the community at large in a safe and effective way, (Ullman &
Zimmerman, 1979). In this presentation I shall state the
principles and premises that underlie this approach, outline briefly the nature of the process, and then discuss how
some of my ideas about dream work have changed as a
consequence of this experience.

PRINCIPLES AND PREMISES

Waking consciousness reflects our personal reality as
screened through historically determined perceptual and
linguistic conditioning. Dreaming consciousness, dealing as
it does with present and past feeling residues of our experience, offers a more immediate and direct reflection of our

state. This form of consciousness, which recurs nightly every 90 minutes, serves our needs while we sleep by bringing into being a metaphorically pictorial display of where we are emotionally in relation to whatever issue may be surfacing at the time. There are certain intrinsic features to this display that enable the resulting imagery to be used to advantage in the waking state. Dreaming consciousness identifies current tensions and establishes significant emotional linkages to the past. The result is, in effect, a direct and profoundly honest self-confrontation embedded in the form of a metaphorical visual (usually) display.

The metaphorical transformation and the creation of sensory metaphors out of past experience, makes any dream image that succeeds in finding its way into the waking state a potentially healing instrument. Once we connect with its metaphorical content it can put us in touch with more of the truth about ourselves than we are ordinarily aware of.

The premises and principles upon which my group work with dreams is based are as follows:

A. *Premises*

Several important premises concerning dreams arose out of my earlier clinical work with dreams and have been further validated by the group work I have been doing with dreams in recent years.

First Premise

Dreams are intrapsychic communications that reveal in metaphorical form certain truths about the life of the dreamer that can be made available to the dreamer awake.

Second Premise

If we are fortunate enough to recall a dream we are then ready, at some level of our being, to be confronted by the information in that dream. This is true regardless of whether or not we choose to do so.

Third Premise

If the confrontation is allowed to occur in a proper manner, the effect is one of healing. The dreamer comes into contact with a part of himself that has not been explicitly acknowledged before. There has been movement toward wholeness.

Fourth Premise

Dreams can and should be universally accessible. There are skills that can be developed to extend dream work effectively beyond the confines of the consulting room to the interested public at large.

Fifth Premise

Although the dream is a very private communication, it requires a social context for its fullest realization. That is not to say that helpful work cannot be done by an individual working alone but, rather, that a social context is a more powerful instrument for the type of healing that can take place through dream work.

B. *Principles*

It bears emphasizing that dreams are intrapsychic communications. Any process that is geared to their explication must respect that fact and the constraints it imposes. The group process I use has evolved with this in mind. From beginning to end it is geared to the expectations and needs of the dreamer as the one to whom the dream is communicated. The communication of the dream to a group is a secondary affair, necessary only to help the group make its contribution toward clarifying the meaning. It is in this connection that the following principles obtain:

First Principle: Respect for the Privacy of the Dreamer

The dream is the most personal communication of which we are capable. The element of privacy is respected at all times. Each state of the process is designed to be nonintrusive so that the group can follow, rather than lead, the dreamer. The dreamer controls the process throughout the session and works at whatever

level of self-disclosure he feels comfortable with in the
group. There is no pressure to go beyond that point.

*Second Principle: Respect for the Authority of the
Dreamer Over His Own Dream*

Dream images arise out of the unique life experiences of the dreamer. The fit between image and
meaning is something that only the dreamer can evaluate.

*Third Principle: Respect for the Uniqueness of the
Individual*

Everyone's life experience is unique. Any symbolic image can be used in a highly idiosyncratic way.
No a priori categorical meanings are assumed.

THE PROCESS

The structure of the process is based on an understanding of what a dreamer needs from other people. His
first need is to feel safe (the safety factor). His second is to
get the help needed to make discoveries about himself that
are difficult to make by himself (the discovery factor).

To insure the necessary level of safety the process
proceeds in a way that allows the dreamer to be in control
at all times. It is the dreamer's decision whether or not to
share a dream. The dreamer determines the level of self-
disclosure he engages in and the dreamer can stop the
process at any point. When the group interacts with the
dreamer it does so in a nonintrusive way, always respect-
ing the privacy of the dreamer as well as the dreamer's authority over his dream. When the group puts questions to
the dreamer the dreamer is completely free to deal with the
questions in whatever way he wishes. The entire process
is geared to keeping the anxiety level of the dreamer as low
as possible.

The second need of the dreamer is for help in contextualizing the dream, that is, linking the imagery of the dream to the life context out of which it arose. This is the discovery factor, and it operates in a number of interesting ways. In the first state a dreamer shares a dream with the group. There are times when the simple act of telling a dream aloud to others results in a sudden insight. The decision to share a dream is predicated on the willingness to lower one's defenses and take a certain risk. There is an inverse proportion between lowering defenses and seeing more.

What follows in the second stage are two different sets of strategies, each designed to bring a dreamer closer to the image. The group works with the dream as its own, sharing with each other their own projections as these relate first to the feelings evoked by the imagery and then to the metaphorical meanings they can give to the images. Working only with manifest content they nevertheless often come up with possibilities that are meaningful to the dreamer. During this exercise the dreamer simply listens and is free to take or reject anything coming from the group. In most instances this game playing begins to open the dream up for the dreamer, sometimes in rather dramatically effective ways.

In the third stage, the dreamer is given the opportunity to share his thoughts about the dream, his own associations as well as the impact of the work of the group. He is free to share to whatever level of self-disclosure is comfortable and thus monitors his own sense of safety.

The final strategy for offering help to the dreamer then takes the form of a dialogue between the group and the dreamer. It is aimed at contextualizing the dream more fully if the dreamer has not done so. Direct questions are put to the dreamer to help identify the emotional forces that were set into play by the day's experience. Dreams start in the present and then move into the past. To give the dream

image concrete felt meaning, every effort is made to uncover the immediate life context that led to the image. The
questions are simple and are designed to help the dreamer
recall events of the day before that left any feeling residues.

The next step further to contextualize the dream is less
direct. We now use the elements of the dream to discover
more of the relevant context, past or present. If a dreamer
has not already linked a dream element to its life context
he is than asked why that element appeared in the dream
that night. Once the present context has been elaborated
through direct questioning this indirect pursuit of the context has a better chance of being successful since the dreamer can now play the image against a more available
context. The questions are for the dreamer's use to retrieve data that might be related to the dream. They are in-
formation-eliciting, not information-demanding questions.
Whatever the dreamer decides to share is up to him.

This form of questioning is systematically pursued for
each element of the dream. When, through proper questioning, the context has been sufficiently elaborated, the
dreamer generally feels much more in touch with what the
images are saying. If this is not the case another strategy
may be necessary. Occasionally a member of the group
may see a metaphorical connection between context and
image that escapes the dreamer. It is offered as a projection of the group member as it may or may not be valid for
the dreamer. The dreamer is the only one who can testify
to the true fit between context and image.

DREAM WORK DEMYSTIFIED

Most of my professional time is now devoted to the
application of this approach to both professional and lay

groups. As my experience grew, I became aware that some of my ideas were changing, particularly with regard to the one-sided use we have made of dreams. The only sanctioned use of dreams in our society is within the context of therapy. The process I use demystifies dream work and emphasizes the essential qualities of the dream, separated out from any particular metapsychological perspective.

The first point relates to my experience with non-professionals in connection with my interest in extending dream work into the community. In turning attention to the community at large we come upon a rather unfortunate state of affairs, seemingly prevalent throughout the civilized world. In spite of all we know about the intrinsic value of our dreams, society fails to meet the desire of many people to learn how to work with their dreams. We have the very limited arrangement of referral to therapy, but this leaves the ordinary mortal alone to fend for himself among the many books and articles that keep appearing about dreams. Much of what is written for the public stresses the virtues of our dream life, but glosses over the difficulties and problems involved and does little to teach the interested reader the kinds of skills that are necessary. As professionals we have done very little except when our help is sought for psychiatric reasons. We could do a great deal more. We could educate the public as to the nature of the dream and take the leadership in helping people learn how to help each other with their dreams. All this, of course, is contingent on whether the skills needed for dream work should remain exclusively in the hands of the professional.

Can these skills developed in the course of clinical work be shared with anyone, regardless of background, who wishes to gain serious and effective access to dreams? From my experience of the past decade I would say it is not only possible but it should be encouraged. In our culture we grow up rather ignorant and unsophisticated about our dream life and a certain amount of learning must take place before dream work can be undertaken seriously. The basic phenomenologic features of dreams can readily be grasped as can the notion of the visual metaphor. When a group of people come together to do dream work and have mastered the principles involved and the rationale of the process they not only will not harm the dreamer but will, from the very beginning, be of help. A skilled and experienced leader will, of course, facilitate the process and raise the level of the work that can be done. But this does not belie the fact that this process can be placed in the hands of anyone, given the stipulations noted. Although there are risks involved when any professional skill is turned over to the public, the benefits gained warrant the attempt.

The necessary skills for this process are identifiable and teachable. Essentially they consist of learning how to listen to a dreamer, to everything a dreamer says, how to keep one's own thoughts in the background, and how to ask open-ended, nonintrusive questions that can help the dreamer externalize the information that led to the creation of the image in the first place. Metaphor plays an important role in our life (a statement which itself is a metaphor) and most people catch on to the dream metaphor quite easily. This process creates an atmosphere of trust and safety that results in a marked lowering of one's defensive structure, allowing natural curiosity to take over. The goal is to create an environment safe enough and stimulating enough to allow for the emergence of the healing potential of the imagery. It becomes a natural and spontaneous form of emotional growth.

The second point I wish to make has to do with the use of the experiential dream group as a training method. I have taught dreams to psychoanalytic candidates in two ways. Earlier in my career I taught the course in what was then the traditional approach. A candidate presented a session in which a dream was reported and worked on and gave enough background material to generate ideas about the dynamics. At the time this seemed an entirely satisfactory way of going about it.

Because of my own theoretical orientation I began to work more with the metaphorical quality of the manifest content and the view of the dream as a communication meant to be heard loud and clear by the dreamer. This led to a number of exploratory sessions with small groups to see how far we could get by working with manifest content alone. For a number of years this notion was explored in the context of one of the workshops under the sponsorship of the American Academy of Psychoanalysis (Eckhardt et al., 1971). An opportunity arose in 1974 for me to teach in Sweden in a psychoanalytically oriented program. I used this opportunity to teach the candidates about dreams through an experiential process, a venture that turned out to be exciting and rewarding. Although shy at first the students came to embrace it enthusiastically. It provided them with an immediate sense of the power of their dream images and respect for the selective and creative arrangements that brought about these images. It familiarized them with the metaphorical language of the manifest content and had the general effect of demystifying dream work. They came to realize the enormous self-healing potential inherent in these images. They also discovered aspects of the group work they could take back to their work with patients. This included learning the importance of fixing a dream in time, formulating the kinds of questions that help a dreamer recapture the relevant life context, and mastering the art of discovering metaphorical relationships. This practical approach increased their confidence and freedom in tackling a dream presented to them.

By comparison with my original approach this way of teaching seemed more alive, more direct, and less complicated. The experiential process simplified the field under scrutiny. It no longer was the complex interpersonal field generated by the therapeutic relationship and in the context of which the dream work had to be carried out. The focus of the work was now on a much narrower field, namely, an intrapsychic field representing the emotional distance between the dreamer awake and the dreamer asleep. The group session provided for a leisurely approach to every aspect and detail of the dream, a luxury rarely possible in the structured analytic hour. The process in its present form arose largely out of this teaching experience.

In working with recent graduates of various training centers I have been struck by the fact that they come away from their educational experience well versed in the various theoretical contributions to our knowledge of dreams but feel all thumbs when it comes to actually working with a patient on a dream. Except for the technique of free association, which is fundamentally a psychotherapeutic technique rather than a dream work technique, they have not been exposed to the hands-on techniques that can help a dreamer work his way back to a felt understanding of the contextual roots of his dream.

At the training center where I now work,[1] the students participate in two dream courses during the same evening—one orienting them to the psychoanalytic literature on dreams and the other to learning about dreams experientially. This combination of theoretical and experiential learning has worked out well. Out of the first they learn about the metaphorical translations of dream symbols by earlier thinkers. Out of the second they learn of the metaphors they themselves have created.

Another attitudinal change has to do with the general

[1]The Westchester Center for the Study of Psychoanalysis and Psychotherapy.

accessibility of our dream life. I have come to believe that our dream life is much more accessible than psychoanalytic training would lead us to suppose. In the course of our training and experience we come to recognize the importance of resistance and the need to analyze and resolve it. We come away with respect for the entrenched nature of such resistance and of the defensive mechanisms that help keep it in place. My experience has left me with a somewhat different perspective. I now experience defensive structures as much more fluid and as influenceable to a considerable degree by the sum of two factors, the real and important natural curiosity that most people have about their dreams and the degree of safety and trust engendered by the social milieu in which the dream work is pursued. As the dreamer realizes that the control of the process lies in his hands, that the group is there to lend him their collective imagination and to help him discover the clues needed to get at the meaning of the dream, as he experiences the freedom to disclose or not, curiosity overpowers defensive impulses and there lies exposed the innate realization that only by accepting the truth about ourselves can we grow emotionally. The dream is the royal road to personal (and sometimes social) truth.

There is still another factor that operates in connection with the issue of resistance. When the dreamer realizes he is working out the dream within a milieu that affords him the proper degree of safety, what impedes his effort is not so much resistance as ignorance. The layman is without any basic knowledge concerning his dream life and a way of working with dreams. No one has oriented him to the visual metaphor of the dream, or how to track down the relevant context. Once dreamers are exposed to these fundamentals it is amazing how quickly learning takes place in the group.

To end on a somewhat speculative note, I have come

to look at our capacity to form these images as a way nature has of giving us the opportunity to examine whatever
may be impinging on the state of our connectedness to
others, for good or bad. While dreaming, we seem able to
explore both the inner and the outer sources of any change
in the state of these connections. It is as if, while awake,
we tend to lose sight of our basic interconnectedness, focusing more on our discreteness and our separateness.
Asleep, we turn our attention to the reality of our interconnectedness as members of a single species. In this sense
we may regard dreaming as concerned with the issue of species-connectedness. From the perspective of where we are
today it would seem that the human species can endure
only if it succeeds in overcoming the fragmentation that has
resulted from the play of historical forces. There may be
some awareness of this in each of us, an awareness that
surfaces while dreaming, an awareness that registers and
monitors our connections to others. Perhaps our dreaming
consciousness is primarily concerned with the survival of
the species and only secondarily with the individual. Were
there any truth to this speculation it would shed a radically
different light on the importance of dreams. It would make
them deserving of a higher priority in our culture than they
are now assigned.

REFERENCES

Eckhardt. M. H., Zane, M., & Ullman, M. A dream workshop
    experience from 1965–1970. In Jules H. Masserman, New
    York: (Ed.) Grune & Stratton, *Science and psychoanalysis*
    (Vol. XIX). 1971.
Ullman, M., & Zimmerman, N. *Working with dreams.* Los An-
    geles: Jeremy P. Tarcher, 1979.

CHAPTER 7

DREAMS: NEW FRONTIERS

Panel Discussion

Panel: Walter Bonime, M.D.
James L. Fosshage, Ph.D.
Ramon Greenberg, M.D.
Stanley R. Palombo, M.D.
Montague Ullman, M.D.

Dr. Bonime: I would like to say that this meeting has been a very stimulating one. I feel the presentations today have been at a very high level. One subject that I would like to place greater emphasis on is affect. I think it's terribly important. I believe that our tendency is to take affect for granted. I mentioned in my presentation that there are certain aspects of affect that one can observe: for example, redness in the face or blushing. You can observe a patient feeling a sense of power when his hands turn into fists. Sometimes you don't know what the feeling is. You just know there is emotional turmoil, and the only way you can find out more about it is by asking the patient. You can't assume that the clenching fist means that the patient is feeling powerful or angry. The clenching fist can simply mean, "God, should I go on or not? Should I face this any more? Should I scream, or should I look at it?" It could be courage; it could be determination. We know a lot less about affect than we think we know, and, unfortunately, we don't bother to explore it enough.

There are many ways in which patients will tell us their emotions. They often think they have conveyed something about their emotions, but they haven't. They will say: "I felt terribly upset." What does "upset" mean? It means there is some emotional turmoil, but it doesn't tell us the quality of it. "Upset" is often a euphemism for anger. However, the patient has not really conveyed anything when he says: "I was terribly upset." Very often a patient says: "I felt very guilty about that." As analysts or therapists, we don't often stop and say, "What do you mean, guilty—what did you really feel?" We assume that we know what the patient means when he says "guilty." Whenever a patient says "I felt guilty," I think it's very important to ask, "What did you feel? What thoughts come up? What memories come up?"; because "feeling guilty" doesn't really tell us a great deal. All it tells us is that there is some degree of anxiety, unless we question the patient further.

Dr. Greenberg: I, too, want to start by saying it's rare that I've been associated with a meeting where I so much enjoyed hearing the other papers. I think there is a congruence of our theories and our work with dreams in 1985.

I'd like to tell several anecdotes and then respond very briefly to a couple of questions that were raised in regard to the last half of this morning's program. First, Dr. Fosshage reminded me as he was talking of what happened the first time we ever presented any of our sleep research at the American Psychoanalytic Association. Roy Schafer was the discussant, and we were using the Rorschach; he liked that, and then made a comment on our observation that one of the things that happened during dreaming was that defenses were reconstituted. He said: "That can't happen because Freud said the ego is asleep when you are asleep." I think you have heard today that perhaps the ego, or the integrative function, isn't asleep.

The other anecdotes have to do with how creative our minds can be during dreaming. Most of you have heard of Kakouli's discovery of the Benzene ring from a dream about a snake going in a circle and having its tail in its mouth. I don't know how many of you know about the sewing machine and how it was discovered during a dream. Singer struggled for a long time to build a sewing machine, but it didn't work. Then, he had a dream that he was in Africa; he was captured by some cannibals and was told he was going to be cooked in a pot of boiling water in the morning if he didn't come up with the solution to the sewing machine. The night went along and while he was tied to the stake the cannibals came at him with spears. He noticed that on the tip of their spears there was a little hole. He suddenly realized that if you put the hole in the bottom of the needle instead of in the top of the needle, the sewing machine can work. And so, one can be quite creative in dreams.

The question that has come up again and again is that of disguise or defenses. I think it's important to spell out more clearly my thinking in terms of dreams being on a spectrum in this regard. I mentioned earlier that the traumatic dream is at one end of the spectrum, in terms of a failed dream. I believe that what we observe in the dream is not a disguise or an attempt to hide something, but rather an attempt to arrive at a more or less effective solution. On the other end of the spectrum is the dream where the problem is not so easily seen. It hasn't been disguised; rather, some effective work has been done. I think if one looks at this kind of continuum in dreams it makes a little more sense.

Finally, I want to respond to some of Dr. Epstein's[1] comments about aphasia, and to discuss the data from a recent study. A psychologist working with us did a very careful evaluation of the dreams of aphasic patients. Dr. Epstein mentioned another study we had done in which we found that REM levels were higher in recovering aphasics—those whose speech was returning, in contrast to those whose speech was not. Another study was done with aphasics who were brought into the sleep lab, and awakened at the end of REM periods. Because they were aphasic, they couldn't tell us their dreams. The neurologic literature suggests that individuals with lesions of the right hemisphere don't dream, because they say they don't remember their dreams. In this study, they had REM sleep; they were awakened, and with very patient questioning, including the use of drawings, the psychologist was able to elicit what clearly were dreams from these aphasic patients. And, most of them had left-sided lesions. She also studied patients with right hemisphere lesions; they also had dreams, which led us to conclude that perhaps the language of the dream is moderated in a different area from our waking, spoken language. I would agree with Dr. Fosshage, however, that normally both hemispheres are working together, and there is not a functionally isolated right or left hemisphere. It seems that we employ two different languages, and therefore I think our goal in treatment (as Dr. Ullman describes in his work with dreams) is to integrate them.

Dr. Palombo: I would also like to express my gratitude for the high quality of the presentations and the interesting convergence of ideas that has been expressed here so far.

---

[1]Dr. Epstein was a discussant of the contributions by Drs. Greenberg and Palombo.

I would like to discuss what I think we agree about, and where I think there is room for disagreement. I think we all agree that Freud's idea that dreams exist only because the defenses are acting to thwart the expression of hidden impulses is not a useful view. There is a good deal more taking place in dreaming besides that. There is integrative work; that is, the juxtaposition of elements from past and present that would not ordinarily be brought together in waking thought, with the result that interesting and sometimes very creative combinations are generated.

However, I think there is a certain euphoria that comes with departing from Freud's ideas that can carry us away. This is what happened to Jung when he realized that dreaming is a constructive process. I believe it has been a temptation for everybody who has tried to specify what the creative and constructive elements of the dream work are. I think it's a mistake to believe that because dreams are not only the result of the work of censorship, that the censorship doesn't exist. I also think it's a mistake to believe that because not all dreams are an expression of conflict that conflict doesn't enter into the formation of dreams. I believe two things are occurring in dreaming. There is an integrative activity and there is a set of defensive operations that are, in Dr. Epstein's words, modulating the integrative activity and preventing an overload of affect that can't be dealt with. We have to think in terms of a compromise, not simply between conflicting impulses (as Freud put it), but between conflicting functions in the dream—between the adaptive and the integrating functions; the latter facilitate the flow of information through the psychic apparatus during the dream, while the defensive functions have a cautionary role and try to minimize friction and danger.

The notion that what we are doing in dreaming is the same as what we are doing in waking life but in a different language is appealing, but I think it is an overstatement. I

believe something different is taking place in dreams.
Dreaming, after all, is much older phylogenetically than
language and many aspects of secondary process thought.
There is something special about dreaming that I think
makes it valuable as a foundation for other forms of cognitive activity. As I was listening to Dr. Fosshage I was
thinking that he might be burdening dreaming with too
many functions and too much work to do. I think that
dreaming is doing a job, but it's not doing everything that
our minds are required to do.

Dr. Ullman: I agree with what everybody else has said
about the inspiration and excitement of this seminar. I felt
it, too. If I were knitting while I listened to Dr. Greenberg,
I don't think you would have heard any clicks. I felt so
moved by what he said, which resonated with the long
struggle that I have had to promote the idea that therapists
can use dreams as powerful healing instruments. I still believe that we can deprofessionalize dream work and reach
many more people by that process, by demystifying the
way we approach dreams, as well as identifying and sharing the skills involved. I felt for a long time that I was an
isolated voice in the wilderness, and I was very happy to
have someone whom I respect both as a researcher and as
a clinician provide some consensual validation.

I would like to address the question raised about the
lack of metaphorical content in combat dreams. The only
answer I can provide is that if we create metaphor in our
dreams, the creation of that metaphor has to come from
some aspect of our human existence. We don't create metaphor out of nothing; we create metaphor out of social images that are available to us. We have a wide range of
imagery that derives from our cultural heritage and experience. But when you are dealing with an experience that
is outside the realm of most individuals' capacity for human experience (which is what combat is) there is no met-

aphorical reference that can deal with it. So, in a sense, the reproduction of the battle scene is its own metaphorical statement.

Now, I'm always interested in what Dr. Epstein says, because he has the unique ability to keep in mind that we have a brain and it does things for us, and that it even does things for us in relation to dreams. The form of dream work is different from waking consciousness, but even the form of waking consciousness—the linguistic, linear, logical mode, is still contingent on sensory input.

Now, by the same token, the form—the concrete, sensory, imaging form of the dream is also related to what is going on in the brain, and not understandable from a purely psychological point of view. The neurophysiologists Bremmer and Hess proposed that since there is no sensory input to stimulate the arousal system during sleep, we transform recent content in our brain into sensory input. However, sensory input is now going down to the arousal system, instead of the usual way in which sensory input comes into the nervous system and sends collaterals to the arousal system. When we dream we create sensory images ourselves by transforming conceptual material into perceptual material to influence the arousal system.

There is one other point. We've been talking about dream function in one way or another. I recall one of the very first meetings of the Academy when we were trying to digest the impact of the work of Dement and Aserinsky. Kleitman, the grand old man of sleep research, reminded us that it is wrong to talk about the function of dreaming. We were discussing the function of dreaming in psychoanalytic terms, and he took issue with us, drawing an analogy to breathing. He stated that it was wrong to say the function of breathing is to enable us to talk. That is not the function of breathing. The function of breathing is to sustain life through oxygenation.

We have learned how to transform breathing, which is a primitive function, into a human, adaptive device. I think we have to remember that when we talk about the function of dreaming, we have two problems: one of these is what does it do for the sleeping organism? Why is it there from a phylogenetic point of view? The other is: If we recapture something that was created during sleep, something that operates mostly during sleep, something that 90 percent of the time we forget about when we are awake, then why is it that we can do something with it when we are awake? We can do something with it while we are awake because while we are asleep we put some valuable information in it that we can retrieve. But, I want to emphasize that we use that retrieval as an adaptive aid for the waking state.

I'd like to end with an anecdote having to do with the way dreams solve problems. Otto Lowy, a neurophysiologist, struggled to devise an experiment to prove his intuition that nerve impulses were not carried out primarily by electrical changes, but were probably chemical in nature; however, he had no way of proving it. Then, he had a dream that laid out the experiment completely, and he received the Nobel Prize for it. In his address to the Nobel Academy, he ended it by saying, "Gentlemen, let us dream."

Dr. Fosshage: That's a perfect introduction to the point I want to make. Obviously we accomplish a great deal in our dreaming mentation.

I was taken with Dr. Palombo's comment that I may have burdened dreaming. If I have done so, I feel proud because dreaming has been burdened with the image of being a very primitive and regressed product. Where there is agreement on the panel is that we are doing more in our dreaming mentation than was understood by Freud, or contained within the classical model. I believe that there is probably more similarity between dreaming mentation and waking mentation than we previously thought. The question is, why do we keep viewing them as so entirely different? I suggest that the reason has to do with the original classical model, where it was seen as quite different from secondary process activity and waking mentation. We still may be somewhat under that influence, and I would like to encourage all of us to see the similarities as well as the differences.

What are the differences between dreaming or sleeping mentation and waking mentation? One difference is that dreaming tends to occur primarily in images or representational thinking, although by no means exclusively; this suggests an interweaving of primary and secondary process mentation. Another difference is that dreaming occurs at night when we do not have to attend to motoric action and external concerns. This allows us to address internal issues more thoroughly, although I would like to stress that dreaming is a mentation process—a cognitive, affective process.

One of my points of disagreement with Dr. Greenberg, if it is disagreement, is that I think we should talk more precisely, rather than only in terms of problem solving and solutions. I see many more functions taking place in dreaming, and don't think it should be reduced to a problem solving activity. We limit dreaming mentation if we see it that way. Waking mentation is not limited to problem solving activity. We engage in many tasks, not the least of which is other creative activities, new ways of organizing, and new ways of structuring our internal worlds.

I think we are more productive at night than we give ourselves credit for. Dreaming is a mentational, affective, cognitive process; however, is it necessary to revisit dreaming activity while we are awake in order to utilize whatever incremental/developmental steps that occur during dreaming mentation? I don't believe it is because things are occurring nevertheless. To bring the dream to waking consciousness, and to apply waking mentation enhances the utilization of dreams. It also helps to integrate waking and dreaming experience in the mentational process. However, I think we can achieve something even without bringing it to waking consciousness.

I certainly agree with what Dr. Palombo talks about in terms of information processing or memory processing. I become somewhat concerned when Dr. Ullman talks about the dream as an intrapsychic communication. I don't think we dream to communicate with ourselves; I think we dream as a mentational process. Similarly, with memory processing, our ways of organizing the world are imbedded in the very act of perception. It's not as if we perceive something and subsequently organize it. Rather, we are organizing as we are perceiving; it's inbuilt, and part of the act of perception. I don't think we should think about it as two separate processes.

Dr. Epstein, in referring to Dr. Palombo's work, discussed the "inhibiting or modulating" dream process. I have talked about modulating and reorganization, but I don't think the two should be paired. The inference seems to be that the only form of modulation is inhibition. That leads us right back to the drive/defense model or the conflict/ defense model, rather than acknowledging that one of the functions of dreaming is modulating or regulating sexual, aggressive, and narcissistic experiences. One form of modulation is inhibition, which is a defensive function. I would disagree with Dr. Palombo, who seems to place an overemphasis on defensive functioning, although I certainly agree that defensive functioning occurs within dreaming.

GENERAL DISCUSSION

Dr. Greenberg: I will try to integrate some comments in regard to what both Drs. Ullman and Fosshage said. I do not want to leave the impression that I said the function of dreaming is problem solving. I would start with the premise that the brain is an information processing organ. One of the reasons I introduced animal studies as well as human studies was to try to make the point that dreaming, or REM sleep, has a function that is an inherent part of that process. I think we complicate things when we talk about how we use dreams either to understand ourselves better or to understand patients better. That is an additional activity. What I was trying to talk about was the process that is going on during REM sleep or dreaming; it does have to do with organizing information, and one of the ways we organize information is in terms of problem solving.

That brings me to the notion of metaphor. George Klein gave a definition of metaphor that involved putting disparate things together in a creative way. In successful dreams, we use the spectrum from direct expression of the problem—the traumatic dream—to a symbolization of the problem, or a metaphorical expression of the problem. When one looks at dreams, one can see the whole gamut of more or less successful efforts at integrating the information in a way that is meaningful for the dreamer.

An example would be the difference between analog thinking versus digital thinking. For example, if you are going to build a picket fence, an amateur will usually take a ruler. If you want 1-inch spaces between each picket, you will take a ruler and measure 1 inch, make a line, and then measure 1 inch again. You will get a very uneven picket fence. However, an experienced carpenter uses analog thinking. He constructs a spacer (a little piece of wood that is 1 inch wide) and he holds it up, placing the next picket up against it in order to obtain a nice even picket fence. That speaks to one of the differences in the kinds of thinking that go on in dreaming. There is a different physiological state when one is in REM sleep as compared with the state, and there are different kinds of thinking that occur that have to do with using sensory images. In one way, it is more primitive, because it is the kind of thinking that we use as children. In another way, it develops as we grow older; we modulate our thinking to more adult and more creative ways of thinking about things.

Dr. Ullman: Jim raised what I think is the fundamental question, and that is the relationship (similarities and differences) between waking consciousness and dreaming consciousness. The similarity is that in waking consciousness we take in stimuli, we process them, and there is some output. I think we do precisely the same thing asleep, except the stimuli are different. Werein lies the difference? If I had to reduce it to one or two words, I would say the difference has to do with our ability to be more truthful about who we are emotionally or affectively while we are asleep and dreaming, when nobody is looking over our shoulder and we are alone. We have relinquished our social role, our social facade, and our social defenses; we take a look at a magic mirror that reflects back to us where our unique life situation has brought us in relation to the issue we are examining at that moment. So, it is a question of honesty. When we wake up, we are moving from a realm of profound honesty—I don't want to insult anybody—but we are moving into a realm where that honesty is contaminated with a little expediency. We won't call it dishonesty; we'll call it "defensive expediency." Therein lies a very important difference.

I agree with Jim that sleeping mentation is a cognitive event, an affective event—it is all of that. But I don't think that captures what it really is. It is a creative event. It is the ability to see fresh rearrangements, to move out of the normal constraining temporal and spatial limits that guide our waking evaluation of ourselves and the rest of the world—to move beyond that, and take an historical perspective that simply isn't as easily available to us awake as it is during sleep. We bring together in an instant what happened to us when we were age five with what is happening to us now. We have a longitudinal perspective that works in a miraculous way. The only way to deal with a creative experience is not to interpret it, but simply to appreciate it.

Dr. Palombo: I hate to rain on Dr. Ullman's parade, but I don't think the creativity of a dream is the result of a miracle. It is the result of a very organized, coordinated, adaptive activity which goes back as far as the marsupials in evolution.

I think the difference between waking and dreaming mentation is very clear. It has to do with the form of the mentation. In waking life, we are basically tracking our relationship with the environment. Our thinking has a chronological structure that is forced on us by the fact that things are happening to us in a sequence. In regard to the outside world, our focus of attention is basically singular. We are distracted by new stimuli coming into our perceptual field, but we are basically pursuing a primary aim in relationship to the environment, whether it is predation or eluding predators, or any of the various gentler modifications of our sexual and aggressive drives.

In dreaming, we are freed from the need for this linear, chronological way of dealing with the world. What we do in dreaming is to take information from two different sources and project it simultaneously on the sensory projection mechanisms. That is to say we superimpose our memories from the recent period (from the dream-day or very recent days before the dream) onto information coming from our long-term memory in order to provide the composite image that forms the dream. The purpose of doing that is to evaluate the congruence of current experience and past experience. Do they fit together? That is the question that we are trying to answer in our dreams. If not, we have to go back and do some investigating. If so, we go on.

Most dreams are not remembered. They are not meant to be remembered when the congruence is established; that is, when we can fit what is happening to us now into what has happened to us before. When we can't do that, we either wake up and start to deal with the dream material as a problem to which we can apply our waking consciousness, or we have an anxiety attack which may not produce any kind of cognitive sequel. The simultaneous presentation of these two streams of information from short-term and long-term memory is what distinguishes dreaming from waking mentation. Dr. Ullman calls it metaphor. Freud calls it condensation. We are talking about various words for the process of superimposition, and the process of evaluating the fit between the present and the past.

That is quite different from waking thought. It has to take place when we are out of touch with the environment, because we cannot attend to what's going on in the outside world while we are dealing with this simultaneous presentation from two sources within us. That's the reason for the isolation of the organism during the dream. That's why we don't interact with the outside world, because if we did, we would start acting out simultaneously different programs for action, the present and the past. That's what happens with ablating the inhibitory mechanisms during REM sleep. The animal acts out a confused kind of behavior, a mixture of various kinds of activity aimed at the outside world in a disorganized way. The disorganization comes from the fact that the two sources of information or programming are being projected simultaneously onto the sensory projection mechanisms. In order to achieve that effectively, everything else has to be closed off, and the sensory projection mechanisms have to be isolated from outside experience.

It seems to me that although this is a primitive function, it is not a regressed function. I think Dr. Fosshage is buying something from Freud that he doesn't really need when he thinks that because it is primitive, it must be regressive. It is primitive because it is a foundational activity for other forms of mentation that take place primarily in waking life. I think Dr. Fosshage is carrying over some of that classical model that he is trying to free himself from when he suggests that for something to be adaptive and constructive in dreaming, it must be secondary process. That is not necessarily so. The primitive function of fitting together current and past experience is a primary process activity. It is what I would define as the basic primary process activity.

Dr. Fosshage: You will agree that it is not the classical picture of primary process.

Dr. Palombo: Yes. It is not Freud's view of the primary process. But within the constructive acitivity that is taking place in dreaming, there is also the regulatory, inhibitory—I think we have to use that word despite its association with a drive theory with which I think we are all dissatisfied. I think there are events taking place that interfere with a pure processing of this material in dreams, events that have to do with defensive minimization of danger and intense affect. The affect has to be channeled within a productive stream as the information is being processed. If the affect gets too strong, the dream is interrupted as if something was imposing itself from outside, and we are alerted to respond to it.

Dr. Fosshage: Dr. Palombo, you are using "primitive" in a different way to refer to foundational; I was using "primitive" to refer to levels of organization. If you want to use it as foundational, that is fine with me; but I assume that although it may be foundational in dreaming mentation, it nevertheless changes. The question is, how does it change? I would say that it changes in levels of organization and complexity of organization.

Dr. Palombo: The foundation is the lowest level of organization in the structure, and the simplest. That is what I am referring to here. I think that there is a simplicity about the way images are combined in dreaming. There is a complexity in the content of the images that are combined that is reflected in the intricacy and the opacity of the dream material. This is a result of complicated things being put together in a simple way. The process of dreaming doesn't, as far as I know, change during our lifetimes. What happens is that we deal with more complicated problems as we get older, or as we get healthier, and we combine them in the same way with our past experience. We are dealing with larger units; we are putting them together in more efficient and coherent ways, but the process of dreaming doesn't change.

Dr. Bonime: I think that one of the problems in trying to define dreaming mentation as opposed to waking mentation involves the whole question of affect. When we think of an aesthetic experience, there is certainly an affective element to it. If someone is dancing, going through a choreography, or playing the piano, there is certainly a very complex cognitive process going on. There is memory, training, and a regulation of voluntary muscle activity; at the very same time, there is a tremendous involvement of affect. There is a difference between someone who just memorizes something and plays it, and someone who can really make music on the piano, or do an inspired dance. There is a great difference, and it has to do with the simultaneous functioning of cognitive and affective elements.

I think that one of the difficulties in trying to make a distinction between dreaming and waking mentation is connected with the fact that emotions are involved in varying degrees of combination and intensity. You can't separate cognition from affect completely. As we try to think of the difference between cognition during sleep and cognition while awake, we have to understand the role and interplay of emotions in each form of mentation.

I think that focusing on the affective aspect of cognition may complicate the situation tremendously, but I also think that it moves us in a direction of greater illumination.

Dr. Fosshage: I wanted to make two points in order to clarify some of the differences and similarities here.

I had asked earlier what is different between dreaming and waking mentation, which the whole panel has been addressing. One of the differences is how much defensive function there is during dreaming mentation. In the classical model there is always defensive functioning. For Dr. Palombo there is frequent defensive functioning. I would say that there is sometimes defensive functioning. My other point addresses Monty's remarks where he talks about how dreaming is different. He said the stimuli are different, the processing is different, and the output is different. In regard to the issue of honesty, I believe he was implying that there is less defensive functioning during dreaming mentation. That is what honesty is about, it seems to me.

Dr. Ullman: May I reply? I did not make a comment about how much our defensiveness is in the dream, or how much defensive structure there is in it. All I can say is that the extent to which defenses are part of what we are struggling with, they are going to be reflected in the dream. When I talk about honesty, I'm not saying we are angels without defenses, I'm just saying that our dishonesty is honestly portrayed; it's confronting us, that's all.

INDEX

149